TRUSTING GOD

Strength and Encouragement for Troubled Times

Compiled and Edited by

George O. Wood
Hal Donaldson
Ken Horn

Trusting God
Strength and Encouragement for Troubled Times
Compiled and Edited by George O. Wood, Hal Donaldson,
and Ken Horn

Printed in the United States of America
ISBN: 1-880689-09-X
Copyright 2003, Onward Books, Inc.

Cover design by Matt Key

The opinions contained herein do not necessarily represent the views of other participants.

Dedication

To my mother and father, A. Elizabeth Weidman and George R. Wood, pioneer missionaries to northwest China and Tibet, who lived and exampled faith and commitment to our Lord Jesus Christ.

George O. Wood

To my mother, who experienced tragedy but came out victorious.

Hal Donaldson

To the memory of Ken Parker, a dear friend, a church builder, and a selfless Christian.

Ken Horn

Contents

Foreword

Divorce rends families. Pornographers stalk children. Illness and disease ravage bodies. Everywhere we turn, we find people facing problems—painful problems that have the potential to ruin lives.

But there is hope. There is one way to conquer, or walk victoriously through, life's trials. That way is trusting God.

Though trusting God with a childlike faith is essential, solutions can sometimes be complex. Trusting God is the answer even when the solution isn't simple.

In the pages of this book, the authors have confronted some of the most complex problems people face. Each chapter contains an anointed, carefully presented approach to a specific problem, and offers ammunition based on God's Word to help readers fight and win.

This is a volume for those going through problems, for those who counsel, for friends helping friends through their difficulties . . . for all Christians. It is even appropriate to give to non-Christians. The answers they find herein will show them that trusting God is the best way to live.

I commend the following life-changing pages to you . . . and to your family and friends.

Thomas E. Trask
General Superintendent
Assemblies of God

Acknowledgments

Special thanks to Peggy Horn, Debra Petrosky, Matt Key, Scott Harrup, Jena Schaumburg and Shirley Speer.

Introduction

On September 11, 2001, disaster and death flew into the World Trade Center in New York City and the hearts of all Americans.

Perhaps an airplane of a different kind has recently flown into your life and exploded. You've lost a loved one, a family member is on drugs or alcohol, a son or daughter languishes in prison, you've been laid off your job, or just learned you have cancer. Someone close to you is dying from AIDS or an affliction of a different kind. Your spouse walked out on you. Or, your retirement fund has disappeared in investment quicksand. Your Christian faith has not met with approval from others.

No matter what your disaster or difficulty, Romans 8:18-39 provides *four great encouragements* for every believer walking through dark valleys or along lonesome trails. These encouragements show why it is always the right decision to trust God.

The apostle Paul wrote the Roman letter to believers who, within six years, would be crucified by the Roman Emperor Nero, their bodies doused with pitch and set afire to illuminate Nero's gardens by night.

Paul writes to them and to us—to every believer who, despite faith and fervent prayer, finds that God is not delivering them from their adverse circumstances. Paul uses words like these to describe our frailty in such moments: suffering (v. 18, NIV), frustration (v. 20), groaning (vv. 22,23), weakness (v. 26), trouble, and hardship (v. 35).

Orson Wells once observed, "In Italy, for thirty years under the Borgias, they had warfare, terror, murder, and bloodshed, but they produced Michelangelo, Leonardo da Vinci, and the Renaissance. In Switzerland, they had brotherly love; they had five hundred years of democracy and peace—and what did they produce? The cuckoo clock!"

What's our encouragement when life is more like living under the Borgias than the calm of the cuckoo clock?

THE COMING GLORY OUTWEIGHS
THE PRESENT GROANING
(Romans 8:18-25)

Think of the old-fashioned pair of scales. Put groaning on one scale and glory on the other. Which one is heavier? Which one tips the scale?

We load up groaning on the first scale. It's so heavy. We think nothing could ever weigh more than our present load of sorrow. We notice we're not the only ones groaning. Even nature groans! All around us, plant and animal life is dying (v. 21).

Surprising, isn't it . . . to find the word "groaning" ascribed to Spirit-filled believers? Have you noticed? The apostle Paul tells us that not only is nature groaning, but we ourselves (v. 22). Lest we think he mistakenly used the term, he repeats it again, "We ourselves, who have the firstfruits of the Spirit, groan inwardly" (v. 23).

But, wait! The groaning is the groaning of a mother in the pangs of childbirth! That's a different kind of groan. It's not the groan that comes when something terrible is to follow; it's the groaning that comes before the great joy!

So, Paul says, "Look at your scales again. You've put your groaning on one side, and it's tipped the scale downward. Now, take from God's truth about the future the word 'glory.' Glory! That five-letter word sums up all the wonder that awaits us as the children of God: the resurrection of the body, eternal life, our home in heaven, reunion with our saved loved ones, our joyous appearance before the Throne of God. Glory! Take glory and put it on the remaining empty scale. Now, watch the scales tip. The glory will outweigh the groaning."

That's our first great encouragement—don't lose sight of the glorious future!

The late Christian writer Joe Bayly told about losing his three sons: one as a baby, one at the age of 5 from leukemia, and the last at age 17 from an auto accident. Sometime later he darted out of his house on a cold winter day in Chicago to get his mail. As he stood by the mailbox on the side of the road, he quickly scanned the correspondence until he spotted a Burpee Seed Catalog on the bottom—bright zinnias on the cover and huge tomatoes on the back.

He said, "For a few moments I was oblivious to the cold, delivered from it. I leafed through the catalog, tasting corn and cucumbers, smelling roses. I saw the freshly plowed earth, smelled it, let it run through my fingers. For those few brief moments, I was living in springtime and summer, winter past. Then, the cold penetrated my bones and I ran back to the house."

Bayly says that later, as he reflected on that experience, it struck him that both Christians and non-Christians feel the biting cold. Yet, there is a difference! As believers, in our cold times, we have a seed catalog, God's Word. "We open it," Bayly says, "and smell the promised spring, eternal spring."

I think it's this very way of looking at things that Paul had in mind when he encourages us with the truth: the coming glory will outweigh the present groaning.

THE HOLY SPIRIT IS HELPING
(Romans 8:26,27)

There are some things we know and others we don't. "We *know* that the whole creation has been groaning" (v. 22), and "We *know* that in all things God works for the good of those who love him, who have been called according to his purpose" (v. 28).

Is there anything we don't know? Yes, indeed! "We *do not know* what we ought to pray" (v. 26). Does that surprise you? The great apostle Paul saying that sometimes he was stumped about how to pray!

Now, Paul does not say, "We never know what to pray for." His own prayers, recorded in Ephesians 1 and 3, tell us his prayers were profound. He gives us a sample of a specific prayer request in Romans 1:8-15. We also know how to pray as we follow the Lord's Prayer or Jesus' prayer of John 17.

The "we do not know" applies to situations when we are groaning, when despite our most ardent pleas and exercise of faith, deliverance is not forthcoming. We're stumped. How do we then pray?

Paul reminds us that the Holy Spirit is helping; He's praying through us with unutterable words. Most likely Paul is referring to praying in other tongues (1 Corinthians 14:15), but the phrase can also be inclusive of an inarticulate sigh or inexpressible emotion.

When our daughter, Evangeline, was a toddler I stood at the door of her room late one evening, watching her sleep. I felt overcome by love for her, and began praying for her. I thought to myself, *She's not aware of my praying for her.* Then, I felt the Lord whisper to my spirit, "George, neither have you been aware of how many times I have prayed for you."

We are possessed with this wonderful truth: in our prayers, God is helping us. Not only is the Spirit interceding from within us, but Jesus also sits at the right hand of God (Romans 8:34), always living to make intercession for us (Hebrews 7:25) as our Advocate with the Father (1 John 2:1). We therefore have an Intercessor in the heart and an Intercessor in the heavens.

GOD IS WORKING FOR THE GOOD
(Romans 8:28,29)

Paul does not say, "Everything that happens to us is good." No, not at all! Some events prove extremely destructive. Rather, the apostle declares, "God works good in all things."

Do you *feel* this? I've asked you a trick question. With all delicacy, I counsel you that your feelings aren't what's at issue here. Several years ago, John Kennedy, Jr. *felt* he was piloting his plane through clouds right side up. His feelings led him astray—the instruments told him he was flying the plane downward into the ocean and death.

Paul does not say, "We *feel* that in all things God is working for the good." Oh, no. He says, "We *know*."

A missionary friend and his family experienced a horrible trauma on a remote Pacific island that involved a savage attack against them in their home by four thugs in the middle of the night. In later reflection on that terrifying experience and the emotional aftermath, my friend said, "We learned to distinguish our *feelings* from our *knowings*."

Note three things about the fact God works for the good in our lives.

1. The comprehensiveness of the working: "*All* things." Try eating a tablespoonful of baking soda. Doesn't taste very good, does it? But, put that same baking soda in a chocolate cake mix. The cake won't taste good without it. Some things, taken by themselves, don't taste good, but when mixed in with other things and fired in the oven, the result is good. God is working to transform all the distasteful ingredients of your life into a final recipe of good.

2. The goal of the working: "for *good*." Theodore E. Steinway, the late president of Steinway and Sons, once noted, "In one of our concert grand pianos, 243 taut strings exert a pull of 40,000 pounds on an iron frame. It is proof that out of great tension may come great harmony."

In the 1980s a terrible wildfire burned over 1.2 million acres in the greater Yellowstone area. Several years later, foresters discovered the new seedling density was much greater than the original stand density. The reason? Some lodgepole seeds require fire to open them. Perhaps a fire has burned in your life recently, but trust God to work it for good, that nothing other than the blazing heat of circumstance could produce such an abundance of later good.

3. *The limitation of the working*: "who *love* him, who have been *called*." This encouragement is not open to all humanity. Only those who trust in Christ are able to rely upon the promise of God's working good in all things.

GOD IS FOR US
(Romans 8:31-39)

Who is against us? Sin? Certainly! The devil? Surely! Death and hell? Absolutely! But, *not* God!

Here are the answers to the five great questions Paul raises:

1. Answer "No one" to the question "If God is for us, who can be against us?"

2. Answer "Yes" to the question "Will he not also graciously give us all things?"

3. Answer "Not God" to the question "Who will bring any charge against those whom God has chosen?"

4. Answer "Not Jesus" to the question "Who is he that condemns?"

5. Answer "No one and no circumstance" to the question "Who shall separate us from the love of Christ?"

It's the very last question, regarding potential separation from Christ, that Paul spends the most time answering. He rejects any one or all of seven adversities that try to separate us from Christ: trouble, hardship, persecution, famine, nakedness, danger, or sword. He's convinced that the six polarities likewise have no ability to divorce us from Christ: death or life, angels or demons, present or future, powers, height or depth, or anything else in all creation.

There may be times when we feel that everyone and everything are against us, but there is One who is always for us!

At the end of each baseball season, I review the final standings for each team in the American and National Leagues. Why? My theory is that the teams at the top of the standings win more games on the road than they lose.

I've discovered, over the years, that about two-thirds of the major league baseball teams actually win more games at home than on the road, but only one-third win more games away than at home. Simply put—champions consistently win on the road. Losers more easily win at home.

When Paul writes this Romans letter, he addresses all of us believers who are playing an away game. As the old gospel song put it, "This world is not my home, I'm just a'passing through." Paul stated it more elegantly in Philippians 3:20: "Our citizenship is in heaven."

The real winners, whether in major league baseball or among Christians, are those who do not get distracted by a hostile environment, or become discouraged when the cheers turn to jeers.

The entire Christian life is one long road game, and these encouragements are given to help us win.

At the end of this magnificent section of Scripture, Paul says, "We are more than conquerors." The term "conquerors" translates the Greek word *hypernike*. *Nike* comes directly across to us as a modern brand of shoes and sportswear. The word means "conqueror" or "winner." The word *hyper* attaches to terms like hyperactive and hypersensitivity. It carries the idea of "above and beyond."

When you put the words *hyper* and *nike* together, you get the idea of a super-winner. Not someone who wins the race by a whisker, but by a mile—a *hyper-winner!*

Take these four great encouragements—the glory will outweigh the groaning, the Holy Spirit is helping, God is working for the good, and God is for us—and win the race of life, not by a hairbreadth but by the margin of a super-winner.

The pages ahead are filled with more encouragement and direction for people going through specific trials. The contributing authors share how to continue to trust God in the midst of such valleys and come out a super-winner.

George O. Wood

1

WEARINESS

Straining at the Oars

LEW SHELTON

Go with me—from wherever you are—to the pages of God's Word and relive a story well-known to most. You can find it in the Gospel of Mark, chapter six. As word reached the ears of Jesus and His disciples about the fate of John the Baptist, disappointment and grief began to take their toll on the hearts and minds of the band of twelve. Jesus, sensing their need to get away for a time, instructed His disciples to cross the Sea of Galilee to an area where they could be alone; rest and recuperation were needed.

It was not to be. Word of their itinerary preceded them and a crowd awaited their arrival. After ministering to the masses, Jesus performed the miracle of feeding 5,000 men, plus women and children. The story that follows becomes a real life lesson for us, people desiring insight and growth as disciples of Christ.

The impact of John's demise had been complicated by the inability of the disciples to find escape; and now they were weary beyond ability to function, so Jesus sent them back across the sea toward the town of Bethsaida. In fact, the Scripture implies that He *made* them get into the boat and go ahead of Him. Jesus would, himself, assume the responsibility for the crowd, but He promised to join the disciples later. How He would join them probably never crossed their minds. They were tired, frustrated, and beaten; they just wanted to get away.

Been there? Have you ever found yourself in your car driving down the road entertaining the possibility of not looking back, not stopping at your intended destination, but driving to who knows where? Have you ever wished you could just get away, and you didn't care where "away" was? Do you know what it is like to be beyond tired, to be so spent you have literally been guilty of overdraft? Not totally unusual. It seems to be the norm for our 21st-century lives. And the story before us is not an accidental inclusion in the gospel. It speaks to the real world of discipleship—not the idealistic platitudes of those who would want you to feel guilty for being tired, or for having moments in which you wish you were somewhere else.

Growing weary is too often seen by some as a form of sin, or at least the result of sin. The theory would be, if one is functioning under the direction and provision of the Lord, there is an energy and a vitality that is like the cruse of oil in the hand of the Old Testament prophet: it never runs out. Not so! Even the Son of Man, Jesus Christ himself, grew weary. It is a human reality. Did we forget that the Lord built into creation itself the principle of Sabbath? And this Sabbath thing has nothing to do with going to church on a particular day of the week; it has to do with laying it down and getting some rest. If we don't, we are bound to get weary in well doing; no matter how well the doing may be.

After directing and dismissing others, Jesus headed for a mountain to spend time alone with the Father. The disciples, no strangers to the sea, undoubtedly felt a momentary sense of relief, having the demands and expectations of the people behind them. That relief was short-lived, however, as the responsibility of propelling themselves across the Sea of Galilee at night proved a formidable task indeed. Though a good number of the Twelve had spent their adult lives on the sea as fishermen, the constant threat of a storm on this particular body of water made their journey much more than a potential pleasure cruise. And their apprehensions became a reality, as far too often seems to be the case. The wind suddenly appeared, pushing against them, each wave becoming a wall of water through which they must push their craft. Now tired, frustrated, disappointed, and threatened, the Twelve hunkered down into their boat, focused only on the task at hand—survival. The Bible states that they were "straining at the oars" (v. 48, NASV). And their strain was not the result of disobedience, but of obedience. How could this be? Why would the Lord allow this to happen?

Consider the wind. Sometimes it is the wind of the Spirit filling our sails and whisking us along life's sea with grace and ease, but at other times it is the wind of opposition that beats against us. On such occasions, there is no effortless cruising, no smooth sailing; life becomes a struggle, and progress is realized only as the result of hard work. The truth of the matter is, though we are all different people in different kinds of boats crossing this body of water called "life," we do face the wind, we do experience storms, and we do flat run out of muscle and mustard from time to time. Wind happens—and because it does, most of us find ourselves "straining at the oars."

This strain, this struggle, is not without its benefit, however. It is in the midst of the storm that we are reminded from whence our strength comes. It is in the face of the wind that we realize the need to fall in line behind the Shepherd of our souls. And it is in the combating of the waves that rage against us that spiritual muscle is built, true character is formed, and pure resolve is realized. We have been sent into the sea, to face the night, to deal with the elements, to wrestle with the oars so that we might become more than we were when we left the safety of the shore. God is more interested in our character than He is our comfort. He is at work in us. He is perfecting us. He is preparing us for bigger and better things, for more satisfying ministry, for greater victories and accomplishments. But before we can do more, we must become more. And so: Wind happens!

From the reality of the wind, let us turn our attention to the necessity of the boat. Now, I am not an expert on watercraft. The disciples, on the other hand (at least four of them), were not ignorant nor were they novices in regards to the subject. Fishermen by trade and navigators by nature, they had no Dramamine in their medicine chest. They had spent nearly as many hours on the sea as they had on land. Consequently, there seems little doubt as to who might have been in charge during the crossing of the sea that night following the feeding of the 5,000. And obviously the experienced sailors provided great encouragement and instruction for the others. But there can be little doubt which of the disciples became the dominant voice in this situation. And I can almost hear Peter, as my imagination begins to create the scene on the canvas of my mind: "Okay, boys, it's time to pull it together. Judas, quit counting the money; we're not going to buy ourselves out of this one! Now I know you wish Jesus was here and I'm sure we have all asked ourselves why He instructed us to venture out across the sea at this time of night, but I have to tell you: He must have a reason. Now, let's grab an oar and work together. We can make it. Stay with the boat!"

You may question the necessity of such advice considering the situation in which they found themselves; but I believe the words were stated more than once. Why? Because some people, in a moment of panic, tend to leave the ship and trust their own power, their own abilities, rather than that of the ship and its crew. And so, I hear Peter's encouragement as a near necessity for their survival.

How often when things get rough, when the storm is raging, when the power of the night is so oppressive and the sea so ominous, do we face the temptation to jump ship, to bail out, to leave the boat? A serious illness, a troubled marriage, a teenage child in trouble, or some other traumatic experience all provide opportunity for the enemy to strongly suggest we give up on the boat and take our chances in the sea. Your boat is the vessel that has been provided to see you across the sea of life and safely deliver you to the other side. That boat is an expression of the salvation the Savior has provided, of the love the Father has given, and I believe that boat is the body of Christ, the Church. And how great it would be to hear the reminder of Peter from time to time: "Stay with the boat!"

Having gained perspective on the wind and being reminded of where we belong in the midst of the storm, there is
another consideration: what steps one might take to deal with
the sense of personal responsibility. That is, unless we expect
the "other disciples" to get us through this nightmare. Picking
up the oars when caught in the wind and waves is the best
thing we can do—in spite of the lack of experience, or the
lack of response on the part of the elements. And what might
the "oars" be? Let's use the word as an acronym to emphasize
some spiritual tools we can use in facing life's troubling seas.

O—*Open God's Word.* God's promises are true:
reading them builds one's faith. Faith is the perfect
antidote for fear, and fear is something every storm-
survivor must overcome. As faith builds, perspective
changes and hope is restored.

A—*Admit Your Need.* Self-deception is the worst lie
of all, and telling yourself you can face it on your
own may be good positive thinking, but it is not the
"oar" you need. Bending your knee, lifting your head,
and crying out to the One who is bigger than the
storm is the absolute smartest thing anyone can do.

R—*Remember Who's in Charge.* The storm is not in
control. The wind is not the ultimate winner. The
enemy of your soul is not guaranteed to have his way.
God is on the throne of the universe; reaffirm His
residence on the throne of your heart. He may allow
you to be tested, but He will not allow you to be
destroyed.

S—*Stay the Course.* Who sent you on this journey?
Where was it He said you were going? How fast you

are going is not the issue. Your destination needs to become your focus once more. And Jesus is not far behind. He is coming to you and will guarantee your safe arrival.

Life is a journey, designed and orchestrated by the Creator. He does not promise us smooth sailing, but He does promise to be there for us when the going gets tough. And just as our Lord appeared in the darkness of the night there on the Sea of Galilee, He will show up in the midst of your storm as well. Keep moving forward; keep believing; keep watching for His appearance. One of these days you will be able to lay those oars down, and you will step out of the boat on that peaceful shore. Until then, remember, it's not about who you are, but who sent you; it's not about where you are, but where you are going.

Lewis R. Shelton is senior pastor of First Assembly of God in Albany, Oregon, where he has served since 1985. Shelton also pastored Bethel Church in Medford, Oregon, and served on the pastoral staffs of five other churches in Nevada and California. He has preached or taught in several nations. A gifted musician, he has traveled as a music evangelist with a recording to his credit.

A graduate of Bethany College of the Assemblies God, Shelton also holds an M.A. from Assemblies of God Theological Seminary. He served on the Oregon District Assemblies of God Presbytery for 15 years. He currently serves on the Salem Bible College Board, School of Urban Missions Board, and numerous other governing bodies.

Active in community service, Shelton was chosen "First Citizen" by the Albany Chamber of Commerce in 1998. He and his wife, Margaret, have two children, Todd and Kristal, and two grandchildren.

2

FEAR AND WORRY

A Word for Worrywarts

BRADLEY T. TRASK

It promotes sleepless nights, threatens our serenity during daylight hours, chisels lines on our faces, and afflicts our physical bodies with maladies. What is this culprit that seeks to harm our minds, souls, and bodies? Many have identified "it" as anxiety, fear, and/or panic attacks. However, Jesus Christ correctly refers to it as worry.

In Jesus' Sermon on the Mount, the lessons from our Lord illustrate that in this area of worry people have changed little throughout the centuries. In Matthew 6, Christ challenges His audience in five areas related to worry:

- Finances. "Do not store up for yourselves treasures on earth, where moth and rust destroy, and where thieves break in and steal" (v. 19, NIV).
- Food. "Therefore I tell you, do not worry about your life, what you will eat or drink" (v. 25a).
- Fitness. ". . . your body" (v. 25b).

- Fashion. "And why do you worry about clothes?" (v. 28).
- Future. "Therefore do not worry about tomorrow, for tomorrow will worry about itself" (v. 34).

Christ challenges us to assess if worry exists in any of these areas in our personal lives. We might hesitate for fear of finding something unpleasing to God and nonproductive to our Christian walk. But the objective is not to bring condemnation, but freedom.

Someone wisely said, "Worry is wasting today's time to clutter up tomorrow's opportunities with yesterday's troubles." Charles Swindoll said, "Worry pulls tomorrow's cloud over today's sunshine." One might respond, "You don't understand my life. It is plagued with mistakes, obstacles, and uncertainties. Doesn't that make it natural for me to worry and fear?"

In response, let's delve into the origin of this word "worry." It comes from both Greek and German and is comprised of two smaller words. The first means "to divide" and the second means "the mind." The English word comes from the German *worgen,* which means "strangle."

In essence, worry divides our minds, fragmenting not only our thoughts but also our actions. Day-to-day activities are strangled or stagnated, rendering us ineffective. Jesus' counsel to us, regardless of our past or present life state, is to not participate in the pastime of worry.

Let's investigate three by-products of worry and three strategies that will assist in combating it.

BY-PRODUCTS OF WORRY

Worry demonstrates faithlessness. It is impossible to trust God and worry at the same time. In Matthew's Gospel

(Matthew 6:25-34), Jesus states three different times, "Do not worry." Christ understood and endeavored to convey to His followers that when we choose to worry we are in essence saying, "God, we don't trust You enough to rely on You." Worry is calculating life and its challenges without placing God in the equation. It not only leaves God out of the equation, but it demonstrates our lack of faith in Him to work on our behalf. The writer of Hebrews states, "Without faith it is impossible to please God" (Hebrews 11:6). For those who are followers of Jesus Christ, faith and worry are mutually exclusive.

Worry produces fruitlessness. Jesus said, "Who of you by worrying can add a single hour to his life?" (Matthew 6:27). Worry will contribute nothing positive to your life. Episcopal Archbishop Robert Trench was consumed for many years with the worry that one day he would lose all feeling in his legs and become paralyzed. He was constantly feeling his legs and pinching himself. One evening while attending a large formal dinner, Trench reached under the table to pinch his leg, but he didn't feel anything. With an expression of shock he said aloud, "Oh, no! It's finally happened; I'm paralyzed. I can't feel my legs!"

Immediately a distinguished lady seated beside him fastened a cold gaze on him and said, "Reverend, would you kindly stop pinching my leg!" As evidenced by Bishop Trench, we too can waste precious time worrying about events, issues, etc., that never really occur.

In addition, the medical community links worry to our emotional and physical state of well-being. Dr. Charles Mayo, founder of the Mayo Clinic, wrote: "Worry affects the circulation, the heart, the digestive system, and the entire nervous system. I've never known a person to die of over-work, but many who died from worry."

Mark Twain stated, "I have worried about a great many things in life, most of which have never happened." A recent study conducted by the University of Michigan concluded that 60 percent of our worries are unwarranted; 20 percent have already become past activities and are completely beyond our control; 10 percent are so petty that they don't make any difference at all in regards to our lives. Of the remaining 10 percent only 4-5 percent are real and/or justifiable, and half of those we can do absolutely nothing about. So, according to this study, approximately 2 percent of our worries are valid.

The U.S. Bureau of Standards states that a dense fog extensive enough to cover seven city blocks, 100 feet deep, is composed of one 8-ounce glass of water divided into 60,000 million droplets. One 8-ounce glass of water, spread out, can shut down an airport. Worry is just like the fog—it can render your life fruitless and ineffective.

Worry leaves us fatherless. Twice within this passage (vv. 26,32) Christ states that we have a "heavenly Father" who cares for us. However, when focus is placed on circumstances, events, and people rather than on our Heavenly Father, worry will consume us. The great preacher George W. Truett said, "Worry is a mild form of atheism." When we worry we act as if we have no Heavenly Father.

A ship was sailing from Liverpool, England, to New York. The captain of the ship had his family with him when the ship found itself in a terrible storm. In the midst of the storm the captain's 8-year-old girl awakened and inquired of her mother, "What's the matter?"

Her mother replied that they were in a terrible storm and the captain's daughter quickly asked, "Is Father on deck?"

"Yes, Father is on deck," the mother replied. Without hesitation the little girl lay her head back on her pillow and went back to sleep. Likewise, we must remind ourselves that in each storm of life our Heavenly Father is on deck.

STRATEGIES TO COMBAT WORRY

Learn proper perspective. When facing a crisis or challenge in our lives we must resist the temptation to focus solely on the situation. Instead, we should train ourselves to concentrate on our Heavenly Father. Jesus said, "Look at the birds of the air; they do not sow or reap or store away in barns, and yet your heavenly Father feeds them. Are you not much more valuable than they?" (Matthew 6:26). If we continually dwell on difficult situations, our perspective easily becomes distorted. Conversely, if we will place our focus on Jesus Christ during difficulties, proper perspective will be the result.

Said the robin to the sparrow,
I should really like to know,
Why these human beings rush about and worry so?
Said the sparrow to the robin,
Friend, I think it must be,
That they do not have a heavenly Father, such as cares for you and me.

The first step to combating worry in our lives is to learn how to keep a proper perspective when challenges arise.

Live for today. Each of us can only live today. As much as we may desire to revisit the past and plan for the future, both continually elude us and even distract us from maximizing "today." Jesus said, "Do not worry about tomorrow, for tomorrow will worry about itself. Each day has enough trouble of its own" (Matthew 6:34). Furthermore, Jesus himself modeled this concept as He lived His life on earth. Interestingly, Christ knew that the cross awaited Him; however, a preoccupation with the cross did not interfere with His day-to-day activities and development. Nor was He hindered by the negative response to His ministry, which plagued Him for approximately three and a half years. Instead He exhibited the importance of living today. He understood that each day presented unique opportunities and to embrace worry concerning the past or future events was a deterrent to accomplishing the tasks that "today" represented.

Likewise, there are difficulties that each of us faces regarding our pasts and challenges that await us. Worry is always an alluring alternative to trusting God. However, if we desire to emulate Christ, we must follow His example and live today while trusting God for the strength that will be needed to overcome the past and face the future. Further insight into the concept of living today is provided within the lyrics of a hymn entitled "I Know Who Holds Tomorrow."

> I don't know about tomorrow,
> I just live from day to day;
> I don't borrow from its sunshine,
> For its skies may turn to gray;
> I don't worry o'er the future,
> For I know what Jesus said,
> And today I'll walk beside Him,
> For He knows what is ahead.

The second step to combating worry in our lives is to live for today, trusting God to help us deal with what lies behind and ahead.

Leave your worry with Him. Jesus said, "Seek first his kingdom and his righteousness, and all these things will be given to you" (Matthew 6:33). When Jesus Christ is not first in someone's life, he or she will naturally be fearful and worry. There are individuals who have accepted Christ, but failed to recognize the importance of leaving worry at the feet of Jesus. Conversely, the individual who has accepted Christ and begins to see depositing fears and worry at the feet of Jesus as a natural process comprehends that He desires to be the burden-bearer of our lives. Understanding this concept will enhance an individual's life and liberate him or her to live a life that is worry-free. Joseph Scriven wrote:

> O what peace we often forfeit,
> O what needless pain we bear
> All because we do not carry,
> Everything to God in prayer.

The third step in combating worry in our lives is to leave worry at the feet of Jesus Christ.

I combated worry in my own life after a near-fatal van accident. In February of 1981, I was traveling through rural South Dakota with my basketball team from North Central University. While traveling we hit an ice patch, which caused the van to roll several times and sent me out a side window and through a barbed wire fence. Then the van landed on top of me. God miraculously spared my life; however, this incident birthed within me fear (worry). After the accident I could not ride in a van without literally feeling physically ill.

In December of 1981, I joined my family on a cross-country trip to visit my sister for the holidays. While en route (in a van) we encountered a snowstorm. My stomach churned and my mind raced as the van slid and careened over the icy roads. Looking out the windows of the van I was overwhelmed by fear. It seemed that at the moment of intense fear God spoke to me and asked, "Brad, don't you trust Me?" Immediately, I reflected on the severity of the accident earlier that year, and how God had spared my life. Yet, in spite of His provision, this fear had a stranglehold on me. The realization of this caused me personal pain, because I recognized that my relationship with Him was flawed.

So, on those icy, snow-covered roads I applied to my life the three-step strategy presented in this chapter (learn perspective, live today, and leave worry), and God instantaneously removed this fear from my life. I slept peacefully for the remainder of the trip. To this day, I have not experienced the physical or mental anguish associated with my fear concerning vans.

My question is, "Are there areas of worry within your life that need to be eradicated?" If so, be honest with yourself and transparent with God. As you combat the worry in your life, He will do the same for you that He did for me regardless of the type or size of the worry you represent.

For 10 years Bradley T. Trask served as the senior pastor of Brighton Assembly of God in Brighton, Michigan, a work he and his wife, Rhonda, pioneered in 1992. During that decade, the church continued to grow and numerous ministries were implemented. The Michigan District of the Assemblies of God recognized Brighton Assembly for two consecutive years as the number one church in per capita giving and

second in overall giving to Home Missions. Brighton Assembly also committed to supporting ministries such as the
Convoy of Hope. The church raised $250,000 for Convoy
and has spearheaded a Convoy outreach in the city of Detroit
three times over four years.

   A graduate of North Central University in Minneapolis,
Minnesota, Trask also holds an M.Div. from Assemblies of
God Theological Seminary, where he is pursuing his D.Min.
He serves as the chairman for the study of postsecondary
education for the Assemblies of God and is actively involved
in the Committee on Ministerial Development.

3

SORROW

Regaining Your Joy

THOMAS LINDBERG

Please read Psalm 51 (especially notice verse 12).

Michelle* sat in my office and poured out her story to me. "I've been through so much trouble lately. I feel like my world has caved in around me. I've been a Christian for over 30 years, and even during the toughest times when I felt like running away, I still kept coming to church. I now think I can see the light at the end of the tunnel, but I've got a question—I feel like someone has put a vacuum cleaner nozzle into my life and sucked out all my joy. How can I ever get back my joy?"

People who know and love God are not immune to problems. Oftentimes these troubles crash into our lives and rob us of our joy. In the years I've been a pastor, I've been asked thousands of questions, but the issue Michelle brought to me would be on the top-10 list of questions put to me—how can I get my joy back?

No one can read the Bible honestly and not recognize that joy is one of the key gifts God gives to His people. The Bible even makes it clear that the entire Trinity is involved in the joy-giving process:

From God the Father: "The joy of the LORD is your strength" (Nehemiah 8:10, NKJV).

From God the Son: "These things I have spoken to you, that My joy may remain in you, and that your joy may be full" (John 15:11).

From God the Spirit: "The fruit of the Spirit is . . . joy" (Galatians 5:22).

Yet, despite all that, it is possible for us to lose our joy, for life to steal it from us. David is an example of a person who lost his joy. (Notice, David didn't lose his salvation, but he did lose the joy of his salvation.) Listen to his words in Psalm 51:12: "Restore to me the joy of Your salvation." What's David saying? "My world has caved in. My joy is gone. O God, help me regain my joy."

Earlier in his life, David bubbled with joy. He sang on the hillside as a shepherd. In his early days as king, he danced with joy as the ark was carried into Jerusalem. But then trouble entered David's life and stripped him of his joy. (He wrote Psalm 51 after his affair with Bathsheba.) But God can restore joy. He did for David, and He can for you. How? Five key words and principles show us the path to walk to regain joy in our lives.

REFUSE

To begin, you need to *refuse*—refuse to accept a joyless condition in your life. Picture poor David. His joy is gone. He could have said, "Poor me. I've got to play the hand I'm dealt in life. This must be fate. I guess I'll just have to grin and bear it." That's not what David did. Instead, to paraphrase his words, he cried out with intensity, "O God, I refuse to accept this joyless condition I'm in. Restore to me the joy of my salvation."

In Luke 11, Jesus told a story about a man who unexpectedly had some friends stop by for a visit late at night. He looked for food in his house to offer his guests and there was none. He went next door to his neighbor and knocked on his door. "Go away," said the neighbor. "It's too late to help you now." The man kept knocking. Jesus said finally his persistence paid off and he received the food he requested.

Let's apply that story to a person with a joyless condition. You need to come to God and say, "I need You to restore my joy. I will not accept a heart empty of joy. I will continue to ask You, Lord, until You give me Your joy again."

For 25 years as a pastor, I've prayed with people and watched an almighty, loving God restore the joy of salvation into hundreds of lives. Their situations varied like sets of fingerprints—no two were alike. But here was the common denominator: each person refused to accept a joyless condition. Like Jacob, each said, "I will not let You go until I've got Your joy back inside me." That's step number one.

RESIST

Second, you need to *resist*—resist the quick fix. David was without joy, but he was still the king. At his command he could have had toys, women, food, and drink to drown or ease the pain of his feelings. But David resisted the quick fix and instead went to God for a lasting solution.

Some things in life just don't work. One day my wife made some bread. My young daughter went to the kitchen to cut a piece, but she used the wrong edge of the knife. She pushed harder and harder, and the loaf got flatter and flatter. It just wasn't going to work!

Neither will the quick fix work to restore your joy. There are a hundred and one quick fixes out there for people to try: pills, alcohol, food, sex, excessive TV, and more. Now let me promise you something—those quick fixes will work for a short time, but in the long run you'll come up dry and empty of joy. As Augustine said 1,600 years ago, "O God, our hearts are restless till we find rest in Thee."

David also resisted blaming others for his situation in life. We never hear David say, "If Abigail had been a better wife, this affair would not have occurred and I would still be happy. It's her fault." He did not whine, "If Bathsheba had been more careful where she chose to bathe, I would not be in this mess. It's her fault." Blaming others for your trouble is a long, lonely street with a dead-end sign posted at the beginning of the road. David owned up to his situation and resisted a quick fix. You'll be wise to do the same.

REMEMBER

Next, you need to *remember*—remember that God is in control of your life and all things are possible with Him.

David was the king of the land. He had autocratic power, servants by the hundreds, and armies at his command. But even though David was the king with wealth, power, and influence in his hand, one thing he was unable to do by himself was to restore the joy of his salvation. However,

David remembered that God was able to restore joy. That's why he went to the Lord in prayer and requested His help. (Keep in mind that Psalm 51 is a prayer.)

Too many of us feel we are self-sufficient. To paraphrase the words of James 4:13-16, we set our plans and think we can do all things on our own. Yet the Lord says to us that our earthly life is like a vapor—short-lived and weak. James tells us that, instead, we ought to say, "If the Lord wills" (4:15). What is God urging in that verse? Don't be self-sufficient.

Back in Psalm 51:10, David prayed and asked the Lord to create in him a new, clean heart. The Hebrew word used for "create" is *bara*. It's used in Genesis 1 to describe God's creating the world. As a matter of fact, this word *bara* is exclusively reserved in the Bible for God's creative power— often creation out of nothing. That's what God is able to do with joy in your life. He is able to create and restore joy in a person whose life has caved in.

A short time ago, tornadoes roared through a town not far from where I live. The destruction was terrible. Then double tragedy hit. As homeowners began to contact their insurance companies, some agents would not return calls, come to the damage site, or fulfill their contractual obligations to help people restore their homes. But God is totally dependable! When the tornadoes of life twist through your life and damage your joy, the Lord God will answer prayer and restore joy.

The devil will try to deceive you. He will lie and say, "You must work up and restore your own joy. God cannot be depended upon to do that." Praise God, that's a lie. Always remember that God is able and dependable to press joy back into your broken life.

RECEIVE

Fourth, you need to *receive*—open up your heart and receive God's gift of joy. Psalm 51 is a prayer, and God answered David's prayer. David's joy was restored. But he had to open his heart and receive God's gift of joy. (Later in his life, David wrote in Psalm 23 that God is able to restore our souls. I've always wondered if David wasn't referring to this answer to prayer in Psalm 51.)

Suppose I send you a nice gift. I wrap it, I mail it to you, and a mailman delivers the gift right to your door. If you refuse to open the door, you'll never enjoy the gift. It is so with our Lord. We must open the door of our life and receive the gift of restored joy by faith.

In Mark 6, Jesus went to a town where there were people with needs. Our Lord desired to help and restore many people—but He could not. Why? The Bible says that Jesus "could do no mighty work there . . . because of their un-belief" (vv. 5,6). In simple words, people in that city would not receive the blessings God had for them.

Many of us have had this experience. You check into a hotel room late at night. You go to your room and open the door. It's dark. Now that room has the potential to be flooded with light. The hotel has provided a lamp and they pay for the electricity. But it's your job to flip the switch. In a similar way, God has provided the joy you need and He has the ability to deliver it to your life. However, it's your job to "flip the switch." It's your job to open your heart by faith and receive the joy of Jesus.

RESULT

Finally, you need to see the *result*—Psalm 51:12 tells us that God can restore the joy of our salvation and the second

half of the verse shows us the result in our lives. To paraphrase, "God will *uphold* you with His generous Spirit."

I like that word "uphold." The Lord's joy is so strong that
it will hold you up above the problems of life. Picture it like
this: You go to the beach. You have a big beach ball. You lie
on your back in the water with your arms wrapped tightly
around that ball. Will you sink? No way! The ball will hold
you up. That's like the Lord's joy in you; it will uphold you
even in the deep waters of life.

President Nixon had to resign the presidency in 1974.
What he did in the Watergate fiasco was wrong, but his
farewell speech to his White House staff was right on. Mr.
Nixon, fighting to hold back his tears, declared, "We think
sometimes when things happen that don't go the right
way . . . that all is ended. Not true. It is only a beginning,
always. . . . The greatness comes not when things go always
good for you, but the greatness comes, and you are really
tested, when you take some knocks, some disappointments,
when sadness comes, because only if you have ever been in
the deepest valley can you ever know how magnificent it is
to be on the highest mountain."

How true those words are. Take hope, child of God, your
greatest days can be ahead. When life seems to cave in upon
you, claim that the Lord is still in control. Never forget, we
belong to the King, and He is able to restore the joy of your
salvation.

* Name has been changed.

*Thomas Lindberg is the pastor of the 2,800-member First
Assembly of God, Memphis, Tennessee. He holds a Master of
Theology from Gordon-Conwell Seminary (Boston) and*

earned the Doctor of Ministry from Luther Rice Seminary (Atlanta). He has written over 100 articles for various publications and journals. He and his wife, Sandi, are the parents of two sons and a daughter.

4

DIVORCE

The Journey Toward Hope

ROBERT C. CROSBY

The disciples experienced the longest Saturday in history, the day after Jesus' crucifixion and the day before His resurrection. That Saturday was sandwiched between life's darkest day and brightest. That week, on Friday, they lost everything they had lived for. Their hopes were not wounded, they were annihilated; their dreams were not shattered, they were utterly stripped. Torment filled the souls of the eleven. The questions. The anguish. The confusion. The fear.

Hope is never more needed than on the Saturdays we face. Something has gone. Something has died. Something or someone that once filled a great place within has left us just as empty as we were once full, just as lonely as we were once befriended, just as uncertain as we once were so sure.

Devastating Fridays. Eternally long Saturdays. Resurrection Sundays. This seems to be the pattern of life so often.

Life is so full of dyings and awakenings, of chapters closing and new ones opening. Dark Fridays and bright Sundays. Shattered dreams and hopes fulfilled.

And yet the greatest grace is needed during the eternally long Saturdays of life when we are caught in the middle. Saturday represents the places where we seek to get through our griefs, our disappointments and to get on with life, where our former vision of what life would be has failed us and we are desperate for a new one.

A DEATH TO FACE

Maggie McKinney, an eighth-grade Spanish teacher in the mountains of western North Carolina, faced a long Saturday herself two decades into her marriage. She describes it this way: "When my husband of 20 years and I separated, people called, wrote letters, came visiting. Some promised, 'You'll marry again soon—and next time your marriage will last.' Others said, 'You're better off single.' Almost everyone encouraged me, 'Go for it!'"

Eighteen months later, when Maggie and her husband decided to give their marriage a second shot, support was limited at best: "'I heard you two are back together,' said one caller. 'I hope . . . it isn't true.' Another asked: 'Are you sure you want to risk going through this again?' 'When something is dead,' a minister told me, 'you need to bury it.'"[1]

There is something cold and callous in the ring of the minister's counsel. Such a suggestion seems more appropriate directed to the headstrong businessman who wants to go back to the drawing board over a project that has failed two times too many. Perhaps the advice would be better given to the teacher of the dwindling Sunday school class. When do we just shut it down? When do we "let it die"?

Such words of counsel, however, seem all too stark and harsh when addressing something as significant as a 20-year marriage. However, no doubt Maggie's array of advisors had watched her on some of her darkest days. They had seen the anguish and disillusionment on her face when she had discussed her marriage. They had heard her grappling for hope. They had seen the tears. Watching her heart fighting to navigate the hurts and hurdles of it all was difficult. Somehow the thought of just being rid of the struggle seemed a lesser burden to bear. Why, it only made sense—common sense, that is.

BEYOND THE DOCTRINE

Jesus turned the kingdom of common sense on its head in more ways than one. To bloodthirsty zealots He insisted, "Love your enemy" and "Bless those who persecute you." To His often-vengeful disciples He upped the tally for required acts of forgiveness from seven to "seventy times seven." And to a young bereaved sister named Martha, whose beloved brother, Lazarus (a close friend of Jesus'), had just died, He made it clear that the Resurrection was more than simply a coming prophetic event.

"Now Martha said to Jesus, 'Lord, if You had been here, my brother would not have died. But even now I know that whatever You ask of God, God will give You.'

Jesus said to her, 'Your brother will rise again.'

Martha said to Him, 'I know that he will rise again in the resurrection at the last day.'

Jesus said to her, 'I am the resurrection and the life. He who believes in Me, though he may die, he shall live. And whoever lives and believes in Me shall never die. Do you believe this?'" (John 11:21-26, NKJV).

Into the face of Martha's grief, Jesus came that day. He walked right into her conflict. Her soul was not only wracked by the loss of Lazarus, it was bewildered over the question of *why*—why hadn't He just come earlier? Why had He waited this long? Surely He could have saved her brother. Martha was struggling with the same thing you and I often struggle with, a nagging *if*—"if You had been here, my brother would not have died" (v. 21).

What Martha had hoped would happen did not. When our hopes have fallen flat and what we expected has not panned out, where do we turn? How could a heart once so full of hope and now so disappointed ever find hope again?

To Martha's stated dilemma Jesus brought hope in the form of five short words—"Your brother will rise again" (v. 23). He brought her a promise, and an emphatic one at that.

Interestingly, Martha automatically assumed that Jesus was speaking in the not-to-be-experienced-yet prophetic sense. She offered mental assent to the belief in a doctrine, one painted on the distant horizons of her hopes—the doctrine of the resurrection of the dead. An important doctrine, for sure, but certainly not one that would make any difference in the overwhelming Saturday she was now facing, not in her mind at least.

Martha answered, "I know that he [Lazarus] will rise again in the resurrection at the last day." In other words, "I know what all our doctrines are. I know that I have the hope of someday seeing my brother again in heaven, in the 'sweet by and by.'" It is as if Martha feels that Jesus is giving her the last thing anyone probably wants at a moment of deep distress—a doctrinal review.

What Martha did not realize, however, is that not only would there one day be a resurrection, she was at that moment standing directly in front of Resurrection incarnate. All of the power to resurrect, to bring back to life, to transform and to make new was in the hands of the One with whom she was at that moment conversing. The dark valley of the shadow of death she had entered just four days earlier was about to be visited by the only Person on the planet who possessed a power greater than death. All that was required, Jesus said, was that she "believe."

Whenever Jesus came on the scene, resurrections occurred. Dead things came back to life. Blind eyes suddenly could see. Deaf ears could hear. Tax collectors offered refunds. Prostitutes could pray. Lame men stood up and walked. And, oh yes, dead men lived. Every moment was infused with resurrection power and potential. All the laws governing the kingdom of common sense were up for grabs for a higher Kingdom and Power was present and at work.

BEYOND THE GRAVE

Succeeding at giving her marriage another shot was something that few people in Maggie McKinney's life had any hope for. Deep into the "Saturday" of her separation, she found herself caught amidst a mixture of conflicting thoughts and emotions. The day her husband came back into her life, she was contemplating the "freedom" she was about to experience, the trips she would take and the projects she could undertake. The divorce papers were expected to arrive any day and she was becoming more and more comfortable with the idea of being single again.

While sweeping up cat litter in the basement, Maggie heard a familiar sound as a car pulled up in the driveway. Without a word, her husband slowly entered the basement and invaded the silence as he walked over and gently hugged his wife. He came this time not with papers, but with a question: "Could we try again?"

In a millisecond all kinds of questions flooded Maggie's mind: *Should she toss two decades of marriage in the trash along with the cat litter? Or should they give it another go? Did she want to have to answer to someone else again? Did she want all the cooking and laundry that went with it? The meals? The sharing? What about the complaints she would hear about her shortcomings? And yet, what about the good times they had known together before everything went south?*

Maggie was not so sure. Yes, for better or for worse, vows had been made. She had made a promise. She wondered about the kids, however. *Wouldn't they be better off with both parents at home?* Still, that seemed a lame excuse for moving back in together. As she walked the valley of decision, Maggie's hopes were paper-thin. Still, she felt more positive about the idea of giving it a try again together than going it alone. Honestly, she felt the risk of either decision. Reenter the marriage and it might blow up in her face; leave it and she might regret having given up so soon.

Hope is the radar system that alone can detect a resurrection. When our eyes can see nothing but what we've lost, hope is the inner prompting that something else is drawing near. Something bright. Something new. Something different than we have ever known before or perhaps even expected.

And how did Maggie's long Saturday end? She describes it this way:

"Our separation taught us a little about what is and what isn't important. Forgiveness, we've learned, is essential. And we've avoided (at least so far) the anger and bitterness that can come from divorce.

"Our marriage is far from perfect. . . . But the marriage is better than it was before. We walk nearly every day, eat out more frequently, talk more. Both of us have learned to pay more attention to each other than we did in the past.

"The minister wasn't wrong. At the time I talked to him the marriage was dead. But hasn't he heard about resurrection?"[2]

What propelled a struggling wife named Maggie to give it another shot? What pushed her over the edge and gave her the courage to do something difficult? Amidst all of her struggles she did not forget *to remember.* She remembered that there is another option after something dies other than burial. There is the hope of new life because of the Resurrection.

TAKING HOLD OF HOPE

Martha's and Maggie's journeys toward hope remind us of a few things that are required if we are to take hold of hope. In a sense, hope is what enables us to get a "resurrection" in our sights when we have come face-to-face with a "death."

First of all, *we need a word from the Lord to hold onto.*

A passage or promise from Scripture gives our hope something to hold onto. For Martha it was in the form of five words. For Maggie it was remembering the rest of the gospel story. With God's help, she remembered that the Cross was not the final chapter after all.

Second, *we need a fresh view of Jesus.*

The Book of Psalms tells us that God is more than someone who wants to simply brighten our perspective about our ultimate destiny. He is more than a stabilizing doctrine. He is a "very present help in trouble." And Hebrews tells us that Jesus is the "express image of His person" to us. He was and is the bright vision of God that we need.

The Greek words translated "hope" are used 85 times in the New Testament. Of those, only five are in the Gospels, 10 are in Acts, and 70 are in the Epistles. Why are they seldom used in the Gospels? For a simple reason: Jesus, the object of the believer's hope, was at that time present with His disciples. Their view of Him and His power was fresh and less obstructed. Their hope was a "very present help."

Finally, *we need to look beyond the circumstances and believe.*

Jesus called Martha to simply "believe." In other words, to lift her eyes above the kingdom of common sense and to become more impressed with the faithful character of God than the frustrating circumstances of life. For Maggie, that included hearing the Good Shepherd's "voice" clearly amidst a cacophony of others.

In the final analysis, Martha and Maggie had something in common. Something vital. Something essential to hope, no matter what day it is. While others, deeply discouraged by their devastating Fridays, have elected to throw in the towel, these instead picked up a promise, dusted off their disillusionments and found their way to a resurrection.

Robert C. Crosby is the pastor of Mount Hope Christian Center in Burlington, Massachusetts (a northwest suburb of

Boston). *He enjoys climbing mountains in New Hampshire with his wife, Pamela, and in-line skating with his four kids, but not all in the same day. Crosby is the author of several books including* Creative Conversation Starters for Couples *(Focus on the Family/Honor) and* More Than a Savior: When Jesus Calls You Friend *(Multnomah) from which this article was adapted. He also was a contributor to* The Lighthouse Devotional *(Multnomah). He is a regular contributor to* Discipleship Journal, Focus on the Family Magazine *and* Today's Pentecostal Evangel. *He and his wife, Pam, have conducted Family Life Conferences throughout New England. Also, Bob has been a guest on dozens of radio programs including* Janet Parshall's America, Dr. Kevin Leman's Family Talk, *and* Robert Schuller's *program. The Crosbys have four children: Kristin, Kara, Robbi, and Kandace.*

5

DEVASTATING ACCIDENTS

Trusting the Goodness of God

ISAAC CANALES

I was leaning against the fence at Lakewood High School in Carson, California, on July 10, 2000, watching our youngest son, Coba, play football. My cell phone rang.

"Dad, what should I do? I don't know what to do. I feel so helpless!"

It was Joshua, my oldest son. The line crackled. I could hear his voice quivering 2,000 miles away on the other end of the line in New York.

"What's going on, mijo [my son]?" I asked.

"Something terrible happened," his voice choked out. "I'm at the hospital here in Rochester. The team members, our coaches . . . we're all here at the intensive care unit praying for Kelsey to come through. Something horrible happened at practice today!"

"What happened?" I persisted.

"I hit the ball really hard, Dad, just foul off the third-base line where Kelsey was crouching ready to come home. It was a screaming line drive. It hit him right on his temple!"

The Newark Volunteer Fire Department had been called to Colburn Park field, home of the Newark (New York) Raptors of the Northeastern Collegiate Baseball League, for which Josh and Kelsey were playing. Kelsey Osburn had then been flown by helicopter to Strong Memorial Hospital a half hour away in Rochester. Emergency surgery followed. Kelsey slipped deeper into a coma.

"Why did God let this happen? Do you think God will heal him? Could you pray for me, Pops?" Joshua's questions rushed out in a torrent, overwhelming me. I stammered out what I felt was a perfectly useless prayer. Then we stood in silence. I didn't know what else to pray or how to answer my son's questions.

Finally, Josh sighed deeply. "I gotta go," he said. "It's my turn to go in. I'm staying by Kelsey. . . . Bye, Dad. I love you."

"I love you too," I said. "I'm praying my head off for you." We hung up.

I wanted to hold Kelsey. I wanted to hold the whole team in my arms and wish the hurt away. But I was too far away. Yet, I knew God wasn't. I called my wife, Ritha, immediately. After talking to Josh, she contacted her supervisor and then purchased a ticket to Rochester. She was there the very next day and met the Osburns—Kelsey's wonderful parents and Chaun, his brother. Kelsey had previously played for the University of Arizona Wildcats. He wore number 41. Josh told me he was the best second baseman he'd seen. He and Josh hit it off right away that summer in Newark. Both boys loved the Lord, both came from solid, loving homes, and for both of them baseball was a passion.

Ironically, the Osburns had just left Rochester to go back to Tucson the day of the accident, having spent five days with Kelsey. They had attended a Raptor game and visited the Baseball Hall of Fame in Cooperstown. Josh had tagged along and the family had really connected with him. Now, as their plane arrived in Tucson, they received the tragic news. They returned immediately to Rochester to find their son in a coma, fighting for his life.

I called back to the waiting room that first night. The guys got Josh on the line.

"Are you OK?"

"No," he said. "Kelsey's not doing well. It doesn't look good, Dad. I have no strength left. We're praying hard. I don't know if I ever want to pick up a bat again!"

I prayed for Kelsey. I prayed that God would hold the Osburns in His loving arms. I prayed that my son would not be demolished, that his new friends would still love him and, if possible, not hold bitterness in their hearts for this accident that threatened Kelsey's life.

One of my prayers was immediately answered. When the Osburns arrived, Mrs. Osburn took Josh into her arms and rocked him gently. "It's all right, Josh," she whispered through her own tears. "We love you like our son." She held Josh close as they cried together.

Mr. Osburn cupped Josh's face in his big hands and wiped my son's tears aside with his thumbs. "It was not your fault, Joshua," he sobbed. "This was a freak accident. You should not feel guilty. God knows why this happened."

For six days Kelsey hung on. Then the Lord chose to take him home. In spite of his own sorrow, Mr. Osburn was still thinking of my son. "Son," he told Josh, "don't give up baseball. Keep laying down that bunt you and Kelsey were working on."

Joshua returned to Southern California to play for UCLA. In a moving article in UCLA's *Daily Bruin,* Adam Karon reported how Josh inscribed the letters "K.O." in his glove the following season. "What do those letters mean?" Karon asked.

"K.O. stands for Kelsey Osburn," Josh told him. "I want to make sure he gets a little playing time when I'm on the field." In a heartwarming turn of events, Skip Adams, UCLA's baseball coach, moved Josh from shortstop to second base, Kelsey's position at Arizona.

God is infinitely wise. He held my son when I could not. He was with Josh and Kelsey and the Osburns throughout their ordeal. He knew the Osburns' love for Josh was a miracle of freedom. It released Joshua to heal and to seek the Lord above baseball or anything else. Josh has learned to trust God in life's hardest moments. Baseball has been put in perspective. Even though he's gone on to play in the minors for the Los Angeles Dodgers, God is first in his life. Today, Joshua, 23, sees professional baseball as a tool for sharing the love of Christ.

A handful of Raptors played out the remainder of the summer of 2000. Many went home immediately after the accident. Somehow they managed to come in third place. Josh won League MVP. But his value to the team was in more than bunts or base runs. Every game that season he led his teammates in prayer in the left field corner.

I now look back with a renewed perspective of faith on that fateful phone call on that hot July afternoon when life had seemed so pleasantly normal. And I realize that that tragic day had been no surprise to God. My son's whole life—in fact, generations leading up to his life—had all been part of the divine preparation needed to face Kelsey's sudden home going.

Joshua Brubaker Canales was raised a Pentecostal boy with deep Assemblies of God roots in two cultures. On his mother's side, his great-great-grandparents, John and Lulu Waggoner, had founded First Assembly in Warren, Ohio. On my side, his grandparents, Miguel and Lupe Canales, founded the great Mision Ebenezer Family Church of Carson, California. Josh would be the first to tell you it was his spiritual heritage and faith in Christ that brought him through that fateful day.

His experience reminds me of Romans 5:2-5: "Because of our faith, Christ has brought us into this place of highest privilege where we now stand, and we confidently and joyfully look forward to sharing God's glory. We can rejoice, too, when we run into problems and trials, for we know that they are good for us—they help us learn to endure. And endurance develops strength of character in us, and character strengthens our confident expectation of salvation. And this expectation will not disappoint us. For we know how dearly God loves us, because he has given us the Holy Spirit to fill our hearts with his love" (New Living Translation).

Isaac Canales is president of Latin America Bible Institute in La Puente, California, and pastor of Mision Ebenezer Family Church (Assemblies of God) in Carson, California. He has served as a professor at Fuller Theological Seminary and has taught at the Pacific School of Religion and Eastern Baptist Theological Seminary. He has been a frequent speaker at *Promise Keepers rallies and other large national events. His publications include two books,* Multi-Ethnicity *and* Romans: A Commentary, *as well as numerous articles in magazines and professional journals. He has served on several boards and committees and is active in community service.*

A graduate of Vanguard University (B.A.), the Harvard University Divinity School (M.Div.), and Fuller Theological Seminary (Ph.D.), he has numerous academic distinctions.

Canales and his wife, Ritha, have three sons, Joshua, David, and Jacob.

6

VERBAL ABUSE
Handling Hurts

JEFF BRAWNER

Wide-eyed curiosity, unbridled enthusiasm, and unquestioning trust are but a few of the endearing qualities of children. But there's the other side to the childhood coin—no-holds-barred cruelty! I've seen youngsters filet one another's self-esteem with razor-sharp words expertly aimed at an obvious flaw—physical, mental, or emotional.

Back in my elementary school days, I had a classmate named Betty who wasn't particularly attractive. I still remember the kids "immortalizing" her in rhyme: "Betty, Betty, two-by-four; can't get through the bathroom door." Like a flower in the rain, this shy young girl closed up in humiliation. School became a crisis she was forced to endure, not unlike a 12-year root canal.

While sticks and stones may break bones, words can break spirits—and the healing process of the heart can be a very slow one.

I've counseled many adults who still bear the mental and emotional scars from hurts inflicted during their growing years. It is doubly tragic when I discover that those wounds were caused by someone close.

Trying to pretend we're immune to the effects of what others say about us is as effective a treatment as putting a bandage on cancer. Covering up the problem does not make it go away. All of us have been wounded—some more deeply and frequently than others. We've been ridiculed because of noses, legs, eyes, teeth, glasses, speech, weight, lack of weight, height, lack of height, hairstyles, hair color, first names, middle names, last names, the way we walk, the way we dress, the way we smell. You name the sore—whether real or perceived—and someone will have felt obliged to rub salt in it.

The bottom-line question is: How are we to handle our hurts? How are we to go on rather than give up in the face of festering wounds which never seem to scab over and fully heal?

The answer we need is found in God's Word—specifically Psalm 17. This practical writing offers some biblical principles for overcoming injuries to our souls and spirits. It is a psalm written while David was under fire.

David was a hero. Songs were composed and sung in honor of this fearless teen, such as the one in 1 Samuel 18:7—"Saul has slain his thousands, and David his ten thousands" (NKJV). When Saul caught wind of the new verse his people had added to an old song, he was enraged. So intense was his neurotic jealousy that he attempted on several occasions to kill David. When those schemes failed he put a bounty on the young hero's head.

David's heart was pure and his motives God-honoring, yet he found himself stalked and hunted like an animal. Imagine the torment he felt within as he ran from place to place, wondering where he could rest and whom he could trust.

Psalm 17 reveals four healing steps David took to cleanse his spirit and regain peace.

PRAY ABOUT YOUR SITUATION

"Hear, O Lord, my righteous plea; listen to my cry. Give ear to my prayer—it does not rise from deceitful lips. May my vindication come from you; may your eyes see what is right. Though you probe my heart and examine me at night, though you test me, you will find nothing; I have resolved that my mouth will not sin. As for the deeds of men—by the word of your lips I have kept myself from the ways of the violent. My steps have held to your paths; my feet have not slipped" (vv. 1-5, NIV).

The first move David made was to share his situation of suffering with the Lord. When unfairly attacked, our first call isn't typically heavenward. Most of us take our complaints to family, friends, co-workers—anyone we feel might listen sympathetically. "Do you know what so-and-so said to me or about me?" "How should I fight back?" David directed his plea to the only One who could do something about it. David sought God's perspective on his problem. He was willing to admit that he was not above making a mistake. He was wise enough to realize that even though his accuser's agenda was his humiliation, his downfall, and his death, it makes good sense to consider the accusation and ask God to reveal any truth it might contain.

When we find ourselves the victims of a verbal assault, God will enable us to distinguish between the problem and the poison. He is faithful to help us make the most of our opportunities to grow, and will give us the insight to recognize and reject unfounded indictments. Either way, the Lord reinforces our identity as His child. He makes us new. He makes us strong. What our enemies intend for harm, God uses for good.

BE WHO YOU ARE

"I call on you, O God, for you will answer me; give ear to me and hear my prayer. Show the wonder of your great love, you who save by your right hand those who take refuge in you from their foes. Keep me as the apple of your eye; hide me in the shadow of your wings from the wicked who assail me, from my mortal enemies who surround me" (vv. 6-9).

David not only laid out his concern before God, he acknowledged his place in God's heart. David would settle for nothing less than God's assessment of his value, worth, and purpose.

No doubt you've seen those trick mirrors they have at carnivals and amusement parks. They're great for a laugh, provided you don't walk away believing that the image you saw was real. So many people suffer needless heartache and despair because they have seen a distorted reflection in the unclear eyes of others and believed it to be a realistic representation of who they are. No one but God should be allowed to define our identity. And He has declared us to be His precious children, His treasured possessions bought with a price. Our value to our Creator is beyond our estimation.

David asks God, "Hide me in the shadow of your wings" (v. 8, NIV). A mother hen senses danger—perhaps from a stalking predator or an approaching storm. She clucks out an alarm, and her chicks scurry around her. She folds them in gently beneath her wings, lovingly placing herself between the source of danger and those she loves. If we take shelter under God's wing, if we let the Lord stand between us and those who would hurt us, what could possibly penetrate His protection?

TURN YOUR ACCUSERS OVER TO GOD

"They close up their callous hearts, and their mouths speak with arrogance. They have tracked me down, they now surround me, with eyes alert, to throw me to the ground. They are like a lion hungry for prey, like a great lion crouching in cover. Rise up, O LORD, confront them, bring them down; rescue me from the wicked by your sword. O LORD, by your hand save me from such men, from men of this world whose reward is in this life. You still the hunger of those you cherish; their sons have plenty, and they store up wealth for their children" (vv. 10-14).

After feeling the intense pain of false accusations and asking God to search his heart and protect him, David surrendered the right to seek vengeance against his accusers. Instead, he calls on the Lord to "confront them" on his behalf. The apostle Paul offered very similar advice. "Do not repay anyone evil for evil," he warns. "Be careful to do what is right in the eyes of everybody. If it is possible, as far as it depends on you, live in peace with everyone. Do not take revenge, my friends, but leave room for God's wrath, for it is written: 'It is mine to avenge; I will repay,' says the Lord. On the contrary: 'If your enemy is hungry, feed him; if he is thirsty, give him something to drink. In doing this, you will heap burning coals on his head.' Do not be overcome by evil, but overcome evil with good" (Romans 12:17-21).

Our goal is not to outdo evil, but to overcome it by surrendering our urge for revenge to God. Even in situations that seem to cry out for vengeance, retaliation invariably creates more problems than it solves.

Paul urges us, "If it is possible, as far as it depends on you, live at peace with everyone." When someone has declared war on us, and refuses to accept a truce, peace may not be possible. However, while we cannot control the attitudes and actions of another, we can certainly regulate our own responses and choose to behave in a way that pleases God.

Paul understood that the only antidote for evil is good. Perhaps you've seen the bumper sticker that advocates committing random acts of kindness. I think it would be a good idea to supplement that plan with some kind acts that are well-planned and deliberate—not to comfort an enemy, but to honor the Lord.

GET ENOUGH REST

"I will see your face; when I awake, I will be satisfied with seeing your likeness" (v. 15).

David's fourth step toward overcoming his accusers was to receive from God a renewing sleep, a revitalizing rest.

I know many believe that this passage alludes to seeing God's face after we awaken from the sleep of death. That concept is true, and a possible interpretation of David's point.

But within the context of this psalm, David isn't writing about dying; he's attempting to live, and fulfill God's purpose for his life.

David was able to go to sleep and wake up revitalized because he discovered there is renewing rest in the Lord. This chased and harassed young man was able to lay his hurt aside and say, "God, because I have asked for Your perspective, because I have sought my place in Your eyes, because I have given my enemies to You . . . I can sleep."

We can go to bed knowing that the Lord can give us revitalizing rest. Psalm 30:5 reminds us, "Weeping may endure for a night, but joy comes in the morning" (NKJV). The light of a new day often carries with it a new perspective. That's why God doesn't want anyone to give up during the night. Morning is coming!

David believed when he woke up the first thing he would see would not be his enemies or his accusers, but his God. That was the view that would satisfy, steady, and strengthen his soul.

OVERCOMING IS OPTIONAL

We've all been hurt. Pain is an inevitable part of life. Some of the wounds we've received have been superficial; others are deep gashes that affect us forever. In either case, God is eager for the opportunity to bring you healing and wholeness. But He will not pry your pain out of your hands if you insist on holding on to it.

It's hard to imagine why anyone would want to pass up the opportunity to have their hurts healed. But surrender can be more of a challenge than it seems. It involves giving up control, laying down our rights, and having unconditional trust. These are qualities that don't come naturally to most of us. Yet, if we let Him, God will give us those traits supernaturally.

Survival techniques and defense mechanisms may enable us to withstand emotional trauma, but they are not the stuff we need to build a meaningful life. There are many options available to us; only one of them works. We must entrust our pain—and the people who cause it—to the Lord.

The cycle of cruelty must be stopped, and I pray that today is the day God can begin using you as an agent of change and healing.

Jeff Brawner is senior pastor of Bonita Valley Christian Center in San Diego, California. Prior to his current ministry position, Jeff was the national coordinator of the Assemblies of God's Media Ministries. He was the speaker/host for the national radio program Revivaltime Presents: MasterPlan. *He also produced and hosted the national television special* Pentecost: The Promise of Power. *Brawner's ministry experience includes pastoring churches in Lancaster and Erie, Pennsylvania. Before pastoring, Brawner and his wife, Jewel, traveled for five years as Assemblies of God evangelists. They have two children, Jordan and Jacqueline.*

7

MENTAL ILLNESS

Comfort With These Words

RON TRAUB

Jeremiah 8:22 (NKJV): "Is there no balm in Gilead, is there no physician there?" The prophet asked this question knowing that there was indeed a Physician—even the Great Healer himself—who would apply the healing balm of His presence to our hurting souls. First Thessalonians 4 reminds us of the resurrection of the believers and concludes with this instruction: "Therefore encourage each other with these words" (v. 18, NIV). It is my desire that you, as a reader, will find comfort in my words and story.

I grew up in a pastor's home and at a very young age I felt a call to the ministry. I went to Bible college right out of high school and met the girl who would become my wife. After Bible college, we went into full-time ministry. Two beautiful children were born to us and joyful times were a part of our home as we had the privilege of raising them. After 35 years in the ministry, we had a great church, two wonderful children married to born-again spouses, and four beautiful grandchildren. Our son was an ordained minister with a master's degree in counseling and was the dean of men at a Christian college. Our daughter worked in our church. Life was perfect. At times, when dealing with troubled families, I almost felt guilty.

Then . . . the phone rang. It was our daughter-in-law. Our son had just hung himself. In an instant, our perfect life was forever changed. Life will never be the same as it was before that phone call. Not a day has gone by in the last six years that we have not thought about Ron—many times, crying out in pain to God; many times, asking thousands of questions and receiving few answers.

We have learned much over the last six years and are learning more each day. God did not do this. God had no purpose in this. This was not God's will. He was not teaching us something or bringing discipline to us. This was not God's plan for Ron or for us. Do not say to others when they are hurting, "God must have some purpose in this for you." He had no purpose. He did not do this.

When depression comes on a believer, it is a lie from hell. Satan is a liar and the father of all lies, and he deceives a believer into thinking there is no hope, no peace, no way out. The believer listens to the lie and takes his eyes off the Lord who offers peace and joy and His all-sufficient grace. When suicide happens, the believer has believed the ultimate lie— that there is no hope.

So hear me again. God did not do this. He had no purpose in it. It was not meant to test us, to strengthen us, to discipline us, or to use us for God's glory so that someone might get saved. God's Son died for all people to get saved; my son did not have to die for people to be saved.

Having said that, let me assure you that God does desire *now* to get purpose for my life in this. He desires to take what hell meant as evil toward me and turn it for good in my life. If I let Him use this, He will get glory for himself in my life because of this. Certainly He could have intervened and stopped it. He could have healed and raised up my son from the coma of death. He could have sent someone to stop him or rescue him. Someone told us that Ron placed his life in God's hands and He kept him.

If today you are in deep grief because of the loss of a loved one, God wants you to run to Him, experience His grace and His touch with the balm of Gilead and the hope of eternity He brings to the soul. If you do, God will grow you better and you will not grow bitter. Running to God includes finding a safe Christian community which will help you share the burdens. We are not meant to bear the burdens alone. The truth will set us free if we acknowledge the pain we are feeling to those we can trust.

Suicide often comes because a person is in a deep depression. Depression is an illness. An organ of the body is sick. In this case, the organ that is sick is the brain. This is a mental illness. When depression causes suicide, the illness is fatal. This is so sad because suicide is always preventable. However, we have placed a stigma on mental illness. This is especially true in the church. We think that if we are believers we should always be joyful and at peace because we have our minds stayed on Jesus. People suffering from depression often do not feel free to ask for prayer. It is okay to ask for prayer if the organ that is sick is the heart, but not if it is the brain. If it is the brain, we must suffer silently without the benefit of support from our church.

If a believer dies of depression because of suicide (never say a person committed suicide—like he committed some crime or the unpardonable sin), we speak in shaming terms. We wonder if those left behind are feeling some sort of guilt or shame. We never have these thoughts if some young athlete dies playing basketball due to some undetectable heart disease. We say he died because he had a bad heart. The suicide victim died because he had a sick brain. Our son was sick and his sickness took his life.

Scripture does not teach that suicide is a mortal sin—with no forgiveness. This is not a moral failure or sin, but a faith failure. Like Peter who was walking on water until he took his eyes off Jesus and saw the wind and the waves and began to sink, Ron's faith failed. My son was walking with Jesus, but he got his eyes on his difficulties, which seemed overwhelming. He lost sight of Jesus and His outstretched hand and he died. His sickness took from him the ability to think and choose. He did not choose to die. In that moment, his sickened brain gave him no choice but to die.

Remember that Satan has no power of life or death. This is God's domain. Satan certainly cannot take a soul out of the hand of a loving God. God's Word tells us that nothing can separate us from the Lord—not life, not death. One noted Christian counselor told us shortly after Ron's death, "Ron's life was not shortened."

I sat up and asked what he meant. "Ron was only 30 years old," I said.

He said, "Ron has eternal life and you cannot shorten eternal life." Jesus told us that if we believed in Him, even if we die, we would live again. What a wonderful hope we have in Jesus.

Having said all of this, I want to say with certainty that suicide is never God's plan, nor is He pleased with it. It is a falling short of the plan of God for that person at that time and for his life. His faith failed. God was there desiring to rescue him, if only like Peter, as he was beginning to sink, he had cried out to Jesus, "Save me!" Jesus waited to reach out His hand and pick him up. Often, by that time, the person has already gone beyond the means of rescue. There were people Ron could have talked to. There was medicine available to control the depression. If only in society and the church we would not make this illness so evil, as if anyone suffering from this illness has somehow sinned. If I have high blood pressure, no one in the church cites me for a lack of faith. If I have depression and take drugs for it, there are all kinds of people ready to tell me that as a Christian I should not because these are controlling my mind; just trust the Holy Spirit, they say.

How do we recover when a loved one dies and his or her death seems so senseless and tragic? We must run to God who is our comfort and our Comforter. We must not hide our sorrow from our brothers and sisters in the Lord, but allow them to comfort us. We have made it this far because our church family, from around the world, held us in their arms. We were comforted every time someone said, "I am praying for you." For months we literally ran to the mailbox each day to get our fix of comfort from the cards that kept coming. Those cards brought peace and healing to our hearts.

When you attempt to comfort someone who is grieving, do not try to make some sense out of the pain for them. Do not try to understand what they are feeling. Do not try to analyze. Do not tell them that God had some purpose. You don't have to have the right words. Just let them know you care. Sometimes just a hug is enough. Let them know you are praying. At the same time, don't be afraid to talk to them about their loved one. I want so much to talk about my son. I love him and was always proud of him. I love to hear how he touched lives. Sometimes people are afraid to talk about him because they think it will bring us pain. Of course it brings us pain, but to ignore him is even worse. There is a poem titled *The Elephant in the Room*. It speaks about an elephant in a room. No one wants to talk about it, but everyone is aware it is there.

THE ELEPHANT IN THE ROOM

There's an elephant in the room.
It is large and squatting, so it is hard to get around it.
Yet we squeeze by with "How are you?" and "I am fine" . . .
And a thousand other forms of trivial chatter.
We talk about the weather.
We talk about work.
We talk about everything else—
Except the elephant in the room.
We all know it is there.
We are thinking about the elephant as we talk together.
It is constantly on our minds.
For, you see, it is a very big elephant.
It has hurt us all.

But we do not talk about the elephant in the room.
Oh, please say his name.
Oh, please say, "Ronnie" again.
Oh, please, let's talk about the elephant in the room.
For if we talk about his death,
Perhaps we can talk about his life.
Can I say, "Ronnie," to you and not have you look away?
For if I cannot, then you are leaving me
Alone . . . in a room . . .
With an elephant.

—Terry Kettering

I am on a crusade to help people with depression or any mental illness to understand that their illness is not a shameful thing, not a sin. There is hope. There is help. People struggling with depression need to be able to say, "I am sick and I need prayer and I need help." If you are suffering and you need a doctor, get one. If you need medicine, take some. There is no condemnation to all who are in Christ Jesus.

If your loved one died of this illness by suicide, you need not feel shame or guilt. If she was a believer, she is with Christ. Please feel free to talk to us about your loved one. Please let Christ heal your wounded soul and restore your joy and peace.

Our family is growing in the grace of God. Our daughter-in-law has married a wonderful man who loves her and our two granddaughters. They are in the ministry reaching a lost world with the hope of Jesus. Our daughter and her family serve the Lord. My wife and I are receiving the grace of God each day and we long to see our son when we see Jesus on that eternal day.

Daily I am aware that the Lord gave and the Lord has taken away. The Lord did not refuse Ron, but received him when Ron placed his life in God's hands. He took him. We rejoice in the name of the Lord.

There is a balm for the wounded, sorrowful soul and there is a resurrection that brings hope. Be comforted with this hope.

Ronald J. Traub is the senior pastor of First Assembly of God in Sioux Falls, South Dakota, where he has served since 1982. Prior to that he pastored churches in Livonia, Michigan; Tuscola, Michigan; Des Moines, Iowa; and Collinsville, Illinois.

Traub attended North Central University. He served as Michigan District youth and Christian education director from 1968-72. Currently he serves as the South Dakota District assistant superintendent (since 1988) and vice chair of the Board of Regents for North Central University. He has also served as a general presbyter of the Assemblies of God since 1988.

Traub and his wife, Margo, have two children, Ronald (in heaven) and Bonnie Hill, and four grandchildren.

8

BONDAGES

Planning Your Own Deliverance

SAMUEL H. JOHNSON

It was a gorgeous North Dakota day. The air around my native Jamestown had just a hint of chill in it. It was one of those great-to-be-alive times, with the smell of smoke in the air from a neighbor burning leaves, and children playing together. In our backyard, I spied my mother hanging wash out to dry.

I was 5 years old, the youngest of five brothers. I idolized my brothers and was always eager to please, so it wasn't unusual, when my oldest brother threw a boomerang out in the street, that I ran excitedly out to pick it up. We were laughing and yelling at each other, so I didn't hear the old black Chevy bearing down on me as I darted out in the street. As I bent down, the car hit me with such impact that my clothes caught on the front bumper and the car continued pushing me half a block down the street.

My mother heard me screaming. She ran out in the street and yelled, "Stop! Stop the car!" The teenage driver stopped the car, bewildered. He had obviously been distracted by all the kids playing near the street and hadn't seen me jump in front of him.

My mother went to the front of the car and picked me up, an almost lifeless form. My left ear was hanging by a thin strand of skin. Like a parade of mourners, my brothers followed her into the kitchen, where Mother laid me on the table.

My father was away preaching. There was nothing like 911 then. Mom had to handle the situation alone. I wasn't really aware of what happened, but I'm told that she took my bloody ear, put it back where it should go, then wrapped a big bandage around it. She put more bandages on my other wounds, then stopped and prayed. "God, I asked for this boy. You gave him to me. I called him Samuel, the prophet. I gave him to You. Now I ask You to heal him."

This was 1944. Mother had no transportation, so she left my oldest brother in charge of the family, picked me up and carried me almost a mile to the doctor's clinic.

Once she arrived, the doctor said to the nurse, "Come, take off the bandages." The nurse unwrapped the bandages, and the doctor began the process of examining me. Finally, he looked at my mother and exclaimed, "Mrs. Johnson, there's nothing I can do. The healing has already begun!" Healed by the power of God!

LIFE'S HURTS

I know the power of strong faith in Jesus Christ. But I also know that life deals an assortment of hurts to everyone—even to people who grew up in a household of faith. I have been hit by a car, faced the guns and threats of communist guerrillas in Portugal, endured life-threatening hepatitis in a remote area of the globe, waded through the most publicized religious scandal of the 20th century and been diagnosed with cancer. I believe deeply in God. I know firsthand that life is often difficult and sometimes filled with pain. That's why it is so important to understand a vital biblical principle: *You can plan your own deliverance.*

A WOMAN OF FAITH

Luke records an incident that makes this clear:

"So it was, when Jesus returned, that the multitude welcomed Him, for they were all waiting for Him. And behold, there came a man named Jairus, and he was a ruler of the synagogue. And he fell down at Jesus' feet and begged Him to come to his house, for he had an only daughter about twelve years of age, and she was dying.

"But as He went, the multitudes thronged Him. Now a woman, having a flow of blood for twelve years, who had spent all her livelihood on physicians and could not be healed by any, came from behind and touched the border of His garment. And immediately her flow of blood stopped.

"And Jesus said, 'Who touched Me?' When all denied it, Peter and those with him said, 'Master, the multitudes throng You and press You, and You say, 'Who touched Me?' But Jesus said, 'Somebody touched Me, for I perceived power going out from Me.'

"Now when the woman saw that she was not hidden, she came trembling; and falling down before Him, she declared to Him in the presence of all the people the reason she had touched Him and how she was healed immediately.

"And He said to her, 'Daughter, be of good cheer; your faith has made you well. Go in peace'" (Luke 8:40-48, NKJV).

People were waiting for Christ. Something always happens when people wait for Him. I've been in services where people stop everything else and just begin waiting and expecting Jesus. I feel sorry for churches that feel like praise and worship is just an exercise, a preliminary. It is an integral part of ushering in the presence of the Lord. I don't understand it, but I know it works.

Miracles happen in the presence of Jesus. Can you imagine the time when He was on the hillside teaching, and lunchtime came? Someone asked, "What are we going to do to feed all these people?" Someone else probably suggested that they be sent home, since the only food around was a boy's lunch. Jesus took the lunch, blessed it, broke it and fed the thousands. Miracles!

Imagine the excitement among the people in the procession on the way to Jairus' house. You never knew what was going to happen next.

DELIVERANCE

The woman mentioned briefly in Luke 8 knew the importance of waiting for Jesus. Somehow she heard that Jesus was passing through her area, and she made a decision that would ultimately change her life. She planned her own deliverance!

The people came close to her, all crowding around Jesus. No one wanted to miss the next miracle. They were with the Miracle Worker.

On the fringe was the woman. I imagine that she had a speech all prepared in which she would share the most intimate details of a disease that was destroying her. Yet when Jesus passed by, there was no time for a presentation or speech. All she could do was press through the throng and touch the hem of His garment. And when she touched Him, His strength became her strength. His power became her power. His presence became her presence. In that moment she was made whole. She was healed!

Jesus stopped and asked this incredible question: "Who touched Me?"

You have to understand the culture in the Middle East. People in that area are hardly standoffish. They crowd and touch matter-of-factly. They cling to each other. With all the excitement, Jesus stops the crowd and asks, "Who touched Me?"

The disciples were incredulous: "How can You ask that?"

Jesus continues, talking about someone with a special need who had touched Him. When the woman came forward, the Lord said something that flew in the face of so much of today's religious teaching: "Daughter, be of good cheer, your faith has made you well. Go in peace."

Why is that statement as remarkable today as it was when Jesus said it? He pointed to the woman's faith as the active ingredient in the miracle she received. If we could only understand this story—and the points Jesus taught—we could revolutionize our world.

One of the greatest needs today is to realize what God has provided for us through Christ Jesus. When we understand true faith, we can take our faith and change the circumstances! That's called *planning your own deliverance*.

DELIVERANCE FOR ANYONE

The story recorded in chapter 8 of Luke tells us many things. For starters, as mentioned previously, *life hurts*. It hurts for everyone—the woman who had the issue of blood, as well as you and me. You see, God is no respecter of people. Jairus was a powerful, key man, but even he had a daughter who was dying. The woman with the issue of blood, by contrast, was just another faceless, nameless, person who had a life-threatening problem. Talk about contrasts!

God loves the powerful and the weak, as well as all in between. He is willing to heal the significant people, but He also loves healing the "little" people.

Believe it or not, we all have problems. The disciples faced challenges. The apostle Paul, even after he had written much of the New Testament, ran headlong into problems that would make most of us quit. Run down any list of the heroes of the faith: Martin Luther, John Calvin, the Wesley brothers, Fanny Crosby, Billy Sunday, even Billy Graham. They all had problems.

Likewise, as with all the heroes, all of us have access to the Problem Solver. Too often we spend time thinking, *Oh, if I was only a minister like that person,* or *If I had his job, or her money—then everything would be wonderful and I wouldn't have any problems.* Wrong! All of us have challenges. Remember, *life hurts* for both Jairus *and* the woman with the issue of blood.

Jairus knew that Jesus was the Problem Solver, because he came and begged Jesus to come with him. Jesus went. Then, in the midst of the procession, He stopped to minister to the woman with the issue of blood.

Jesus doesn't go with you or stop for you because of your position in life, nor is He impressed because of your education, nor does He judge you because of where you come from. He receives you just as you are. He receives you even if you have failed miserably as a young person. He receives you with one failed marriage, many failed marriages or if you have never been married. He receives the drug addict, the murderer and the innocent child. He receives each of us just as we are.

Society doesn't do that.

Our families don't always do that.

The church doesn't do it.

Neighbors don't do it.

But Jesus does. When we come to Him with an honest heart, He receives us just as we are.

APPLICATION

Either God's Word is true or it isn't. God will either do what He has promised, or He will not do it. The promises of God are either reliable or they aren't.

The sad fact is that unbelief is keeping back God's richest blessing on His people today. Unbelief holds back God's miracles. Can you imagine what would happen if His own people would stop holding back revival? Doubtless there would be more people saved than ever before, since the Lord only manifests himself to faith and not to unbelief. He refuses to work unless people believe Him first. He will not work for us when we make Him out to be a liar by not believing His Word.

Unbelief is the opposite of faith. If you desire to move forward in faith and plan your own deliverance, you cannot continue in unbelief. It is only where God finds the exercise of living faith that He can work.

Now it's time to do something about it. You must *plan your deliverance*, just as the dying woman said, "If only I may touch His garment, I shall be made well" (Matthew 9:21).

Are you facing a financial crisis? Do you need healing in your body? Are there unsaved loved ones? Remember faith is the active ingredient that opens the windows of heaven. Jesus said so. You and I determine deep down inside. That's where faith begins.

"For she said to herself...." That's where it starts. Press through and touch Jesus and be made whole!

Sam Johnson has served as a pastor, missionary and missionary statesman, as well as the director of a worldwide television ministry reaching into 50 countries. From 1987-1993, he served as pastor of Crown Christian Center in Charlotte, North Carolina, in addition to ministering across America via radio and television.

Today, Johnson assists the missionaries and nationals of Eastern Europe in establishing Bible schools and training centers. From his experience as a missionary in Europe for 20 years, during which he served as the European missions director for seven years, he knows the value of training nationals to reach their own people.

Johnson serves as the vice president of Mission of Mercy, serving Europe and Africa. In cooperation with the Assemblies of God, Mission of Mercy not only ministers in India, Bangladesh, Cambodia, Laos and Vietnam, but today is building an orphanage, vocational school, clinic and family life center in Romania and in Ethiopia.

Johnson conducts missions and evangelistic crusades across America 45 weeks of the year. He conducts crusades in Europe the remaining weeks available. He also shares how individuals can become involved in reaching the hurting of our world for Jesus Christ.

Johnson and his wife, Joyce, live in Minneapolis, Minnesota, and have three grown sons.

9

PORNOGRAPHY

An Attack of the Enemy

DAVID W. ARGUE

Pornography is one of the most insidious attacks of the enemy against the church of Jesus Christ. Pornography is an immoral, illicit depiction of erotic behavior via words, pictures, videos, drawings or people intended to arouse improper sexual feelings or responses in the person reading or viewing the medium. Pornography is found on television, in magazines, in paperbacks, in novels, in lingerie catalogs, on the Internet. We are plagued by lust and sensuality.

Jesus lived purely and spoke clearly about lust. He said, "You know the commandment which says, 'Be faithful in marriage.' But I tell you that if you look at another woman and want her, you are already unfaithful in your thoughts" (Matthew 5:27,28, CEV).

How do luring looks corrupt? Here are six stages:

STAGE 1. TEMPTATION

If the temptation to read or view pornography is not resisted, urges mount and voices entice: "You need to experience this excitement." "You need to explore the intimate without the responsibility of relating to a real person." "You need to be informed." Research shows that when the imagination and the will conflict, the imagination almost always wins. The battle must be won in the realm of the imagination. We need to watch over our minds and our eyes.

Say it out loud. Say it under your breath. Say it as you drive the car. When the enemy mounts an attack against your mind, say, "No, Lord Jesus, this is not for me." James says, "Resist the devil, and he will flee from you" (James 4:7, NIV). Resist at the earliest possible moment. A temptation, if not resisted, becomes an encounter.

STAGE 2. ENCOUNTER

James says, "After desire has conceived, it gives birth to sin; and sin, when it is full-grown, gives birth to death" (James 1:15). Pornography has an impact on the mind, the body and the spirit all at the same time. A linkage is established between pornography and hormonal release. Just one encounter can signal the beginning for some of a pattern that can lead quickly to the next stage.

STAGE 3. ADDICTION

Pornography is addictive in the same way that heroin and crack are addictive. Dr. James Mago of the University of

California says, "Experiences at the time of emotional or sexual arousal get locked in the brain chemically and become very difficult to erase." Jesus said, "Everyone who sins [continually] is a slave to sin" (John 8:34). No resistance to an encounter leads to addiction. And with no redemption or rescue, the next stage is reached.

STAGE 4. ESCALATION

Pornography involves sexual stimulation without real satisfaction. It involves sexual excitement without personal fulfillment. Pornography abuses the most intimate dimension of life. Satan uses the immoral to take more and more from the soul and body and mind of a person, while giving less and less of the erotic buzz he or she desires. So a person addicted to pornography finds it increasingly difficult to achieve the same level of stimulation. Stronger, usually more degenerate and even brutalizing forms of stimulation are needed.

The Bible talks about escalation: "Their foolish hearts were darkened. . . . God gave them over to shameful lusts. . . . [They] were inflamed with lust. . . . [God] gave them over to a depraved mind. . . . They not only continue to do these very things but also approve of those who practice them" (Romans 1:21-32). Then comes the desensitization stage.

STAGE 5. DESENSITIZATION

What at first shocked and disgusted a person is now deemed acceptable. The conscience, having become seared as with a "hot iron" (1 Timothy 4:2), is impaired to the point of tolerating gross immorality. Tests involving college students showed that, after exposure to "soft" pornography for a limited number of hours, their reaction to nudity and rape were dulled. Once this stage has passed, we sometimes read about the consequences on the front page of the daily newspaper.

STAGE 6. ACTING OUT

In this stage, a person moves from being tempted to do immoral acts, to actually doing them. Ideas, pictures, thoughts, and suggestions put into the mind are acted out. Input produces expression. Jesus said, "The evil man brings evil things out of the evil stored up in his heart" (Luke 6:45).

God intends that sexual intimacy be reserved for the privacy of marriage. If you are not doing well with your intimate relationship, pray and talk to your spouse. In the midst of your gadgets, pray for great godliness. In the midst of your sophistication, may the Spirit grant great power and great glory that will drive holiness and sanctification and purity and caution and care into your heart and spirit.

TWO STEPS TO FREEDOM

Here are two steps that will assist anyone who has been involved in pornography in any degree.

Come clean. Walk through each element where pornography has affected you and repent before God for all of it. Turn your entire person over to Christ—your thought life, your sex life, your emotional life.

Read Proverbs and find 25 references to the issue of pornography.

Live clean. Take inventory of the filth in your life and get rid of it. Don't channel surf. If cable television is an inroad of the enemy into your life, get rid of it. Jesus said, "If your right eye causes you to sin, gouge it out and throw it away. It is better for you to lose one part of your body than for your whole body to be thrown into hell" (Matthew 5:29). I say, "If your cable network offends you, disengage it. Because it's better to go through life without cable than into hell with your cable memory."

I travel a lot. When I arrive in my hotel room, I call home and report that I've unplugged the TV. At times I tape pictures of my wife and family over the TV screen.

Become accountable to someone who is aware of your struggle. Urge that person to ask you periodically, "How are you doing?"

The reason Jesus came was to destroy the devil's work, including pornography. And that's what He will do for all who let Him.

David W. Argue is founding pastor of Christ's Place (Assemblies of God) in Lincoln, Nebraska, and is an executive presbyter of the Assemblies of God. He has served on numerous boards and commissions, including Global University, North Central University, and the World Missions and Home Missions boards of the Assemblies of God.

A graduate of Central Bible College, Wheaton College, and the University of Nebraska, Argue has traveled nationwide and to several nations in ministry. He has published numerous articles and has contributed to such books as The Pentecostal Pastor.

He and his wife, Jackie, have five children and four grandchildren. Married in 1994 after both had been widowed, they minister frequently together on marriage and ministry.

10

FAILURE

Bouncing Back

RAY BERRYHILL

"Though a righteous man falls seven times, he rises again" (Proverbs 24:16, NIV). Failure is a word we don't like to use when describing ourselves, but it's a word that often applies to our lives. I was 21 when feelings of failure nearly over-whelmed me. I was asked to leave the church my grand-mother helped to pioneer, but in the end I would learn a valuable lesson that would benefit me even today.

At the age of 5, I realized God's hand was on my life. I remember "playing church" by myself in my bedroom. I remember acting like an usher and welcoming imaginary people into the house of God (my bedroom). I remember praying like the deacons, bowing on my knees and calling on God. I remember singing as if in the choir, and making the bedsheets my choir robe. I remember singing praises to God and actually feeling His presence in my room. I remember "tuning up" like my pastor, and "preaching 'bout the good-ness of the Lawd" to all the imaginary people. Even then I knew God was going to use me.

I came to know Jesus as my personal Savior at the age of 14. I was coming home from my grandmother's church, and a Pentecostal missionary named Mary Everett was preaching the gospel on the street. This was the first time I heard about asking Jesus to forgive my sins and come into my heart. So, in response to the message, I did it, and just as the Word says, I became a new creation.

Before long I began following Sister Everett. She taught me how to pray, how to believe God, and how to live holy. She taught me about the power of the Holy Ghost. Sister Everett saw things in me I couldn't see in myself. She spoke purpose and destiny into my life and when she called me a "natural born leader" and "man of God," I began to believe it.

I told her I was going to leave my church to become Pentecostal. But she said I could live holy anywhere and that if I would walk upright and be a light before the people in my church, I would win them too. I went back to my church and just began to live right. At first, they mocked me and called me names. But I didn't care. They thought I was going through a change; in actuality a change had gone through me.

The young people began to ask me to teach them the Word of God. As I would have prayer and Bible studies most of them repented and accepted Jesus. But then the unexpect-ed happened—when they got saved, their parents did too. Then I got filled with the Holy Ghost, speaking in other tongues. So did they, and some of their parents as well. The baptism in the Holy Spirit became the gateway to other spiritual gifts being manifested in our midst. Over the next several years, we experienced the power of God in unimaginable ways.

Who would have thought that in Cabrini Green, one of the most notorious housing projects in Chicago—and the nation—there would be a move of God with salvations, healings, miracles, and instantaneous deliverances from sin and Satan? Through a small group of young people, a church experienced the power of the gospel transforming individuals, families, and a community.

But even with this phenomenon, I encountered failure head-on. Sister Everett passed away. I was without a mentor. In the midst of a powerful revival, I didn't know how to facilitate a move of God. I foolishly thought that as long as God was moving, everything was all right. What I failed to realize was even a move of God, if not handled properly, could "give place to the devil."

The people at my church were good people. We were like a close-knit family. But while some were hungry for God, others didn't have a clue as to what was happening. The church had become divided between those who just came to church, but were ignorant of the truth, and those who had experienced the truth, but looked down on anyone who hadn't. We were like Israel, who had "a zeal of God, but not according to knowledge" (Romans 10:2, KJV).

In my zeal, I led most of those people to the Lord. Even today, many of them are pastors, evangelists and teachers scattered throughout the country. I helped to replace dead traditions and empty religion with a solid biblical foundation for them to grow on. I fashioned an award-winning choir— one of the finest in Chicago. I provided leadership that saw the church grow from less than 100 to more than 300.

But crises resulted because I didn't know how to manage what was taking place. I didn't know how to reconcile a divided congregation. I didn't know how to deal with self-righteous Christians, including myself. And worst of all, I didn't know how to process the failures of our pastor, who in addition to being deficient in his understanding and application of the Word, was immoral—and had no desire to change.

I honestly thought I could help to change him. I believed that somehow, if I lived right, even my pastor would get right. Apparent personal success and the support of other people caused me to believe I was the leader, when clearly the pastor was the set man of the house, the one God anointed to lead that church.

When he didn't change, without realizing it, I judged and disrespected him. In ignorance, I would speak against him. In pride, I resisted his teachings. In private, I would mock him. Subtly I would challenge him and rebel against his authority. Thus, in the midst of an unprecedented move of God, I was told to leave my grandmother's church . . . and I was devastated.

I could have spiritualized it by saying, "He just didn't want the move of God." I could have trivialized it by saying, "He was just intimidated by how God was using me." But this church had been my life. It was my grandmother's church—my mother's church! I thought I would be there forever, and probably become the next pastor. But after a time of prayer I sensed the peace of God, and knew this was His will.

I could have responded in many ways. I could have told everybody the things my pastor said in private. I could have urged the deacons to call a church meeting. I had enough influence to split that church into pieces and walk away with the majority of the membership.

But the reality is, despite all that was accomplished, I had failed! I failed to obey the Scriptures concerning God's people and, particularly, leaders.

First Chronicles 16:22 says, "Touch not mine anointed, and do my prophets no harm." First Timothy 5:1: "Rebuke not an elder, but entreat him as a father." First Thessalonians 5:12 commands honor to those over you. I had "touched," and rebuked, and had failed to honor the man of God. It didn't matter that he was wrong. I should have honored the office, even when I couldn't honor the man.

My retaliation was against his immorality and other indiscretions. But it was not my place to retaliate. "Vengeance is mine . . . saith the Lord" (Romans 12:19). Nor was it my place to correct him. Nor was it my place to rebel against his authority. Nor was it my place to expose him. I wasn't in a position of authority, and the systems of accountability we benefit from today were not yet in place.

The only honorable and appropriate decision for me was to leave the church. But I couldn't bring myself to do it. Even though I wasn't being fed. Even though I was giving more than I was receiving. Even though I "knew" that my pastor wasn't living righteously. So, since I wouldn't leave, God allowed me to be put out.

The very next Sunday, without prior notice to anyone, I resigned publicly. I honored my pastor, thanked the congregation for the privilege to minister among them, acknowledged God's will and timing for leaving and left respectably with the blessing of the church. Although many questions were raised I refused to talk about it any further. First Corinthians 3:17

warns that whoever destroys the church will himself be destroyed by God. To speak of it would've caused more division, and I knew God wouldn't honor splitting a church.

Over the years I served at other churches, and found myself in the same dilemma. I would join, God would use me, the congregation would embrace me, the pastor would affirm me, God would bless the work, and the pastor would later despise me, just as Saul despised David.

But the difference was I had learned my lessons well. I learned it was never my place to come against the pastor. The pastor was accountable to the Lord and to those in authority, not to me. I learned the anointing runs down not up. If God doesn't anoint the pastor, he certainly won't be anointed by anyone else. I learned that you only grow to the level of leadership to which you are submitted. I learned when I could no longer submit to leadership, to depart amicably without dissension. And because God helped me leave the churches I attended respectfully, I am welcome today to come back—including to my grandmother's church. I bounced back from failure! I'll never fail this way again!

This experience taught me a lot about failure.

First, failure is part of the growth process. From the Scriptures we see that Abraham, Moses, Samson, David, Peter, and John Mark all grew as a result of failure.

Second, the world views failure as the lack of accomplishment, while God views failure as living without Him. When we attempt to live without God, He simply withdraws His blessing, which results in diminished position, diminished power, diminished wealth, diminished honor, and ultimately a broken relationship with God.

But when you stay with God, failure is neither fatal nor final because His grace will be there to meet you at your point of failure.

Micah 7:8,9 says, "Rejoice not against me, O mine enemy: when I fall, I shall arise; when I sit in darkness, the Lord shall be a light unto me. I will bear the indignation of the Lord, because I have sinned against him, until he plead my cause, and execute judgment for me: he will bring me forth to the light, and I shall behold his righteousness."

Lastly, it has been said, "True success is born out of failure." Despite innumerable failures, today I'm a blessed man. My wife and I and our seven children are all serving the Lord. I have the privilege of pastoring a thriving, diverse congregation that loves God and is abounding in Him. The ministry has surpassed that of my teachers', and even my own expectations. God is honoring the work of our hands with souls, godly character, and good works.

But it's through failure that I've come to know the ways of the Lord. Before I failed, I thought success was all about achievement. But having failed so many times, I see it as a great teacher.

Failure taught me the truth about myself.

Failure taught me the pointlessness of arrogance.

Failure taught me to seek God for truthful answers.

Failure taught me to be sensitive to others who have failed.

May you be encouraged and know that failing doesn't make you a failure. Even in your failure God extends His hand to lift you up.

"The steps of good men are directed by the Lord. He delights in each step they take. If they fall it isn't fatal, for the Lord holds them with his hand" (Psalm 37:23,24, LB).

Ray Allen Berryhill, Sr. has been the senior pastor of Evangel Assembly of God in Chicago since 1992, following four years as music pastor there. Prior to that he served three other churches as associate minister and/or minister of music. From 1981 to 1992 he also traveled in itinerant music ministry.

Berryhill has served on numerous boards and committees for the General Council of the Assemblies of God, the Illinois District Council, the National Black Fellowship and the Chicago Central Section of the Illinois District. He has served as a conference speaker, and/or worship leader for the General Council, for numerous Sectional and District Councils, and for churches, universities and ministry organizations around the country. He performed, along with the Evangel Celebration Choir, for the 1995 General Council in St. Louis, Missouri; the 1997 General Council, Indianapolis, Indiana; and in the lead role of William Seymour, in Touch Felt 'Round the World, for the 2000 Celebration/World Congress in Indianapolis. He also appears regularly on radio and television and has several recordings to his credit.

Berryhill attended Moody Bible Institute and Chicago Baptist Institute. He and his wife, Adrienne Denise, have seven children—four of their own, Ray Jr., Jeremy, Wesley, and Micah Berryhill; and three adopted, Michael, Joshuah, and Amelia Butts.

11

FINANCES

Four Steps to Financial Freedom

BILL BUCHHOLZ

It was the spring of '64.

A few months earlier JFK had been shot in Dallas. Things were returning to normal in my elementary school. I was just a normal, goofy-looking kid with freckles and Brylcream in my hair. I loved sports. I loved freedom. McDonald's was new in my neighborhood. I could not afford the 15-cent hamburger or the 12-cent french fries. How could I possibly scrape enough money together?

I got creative. I took the 35 cents my mom gave me for the school cafeteria, rode my bike to the Rexall drugstore during lunch break twice each week, spent all my lunch money for licorice at a penny a piece, then came back to school and sold my licorice to kids on the playground, two for a nickel. I made 80 cents a day, and was able to afford a trip to McDonald's once a week and still have money left over.

To get that burger and fries I had to miss some of the lunches I wanted at school. It was more than sacrifice. I actually had to eat licorice for lunch a couple of days a week! Candy tastes great to a kid, but you sure get hungry before dinner when that's all you eat during the day. We laugh about it now, my parents and I. But in some ways my mom and dad are proud. Not because I cut lunch; but because I learned the importance of delayed gratification and coming up with a plan instead of accepting things the way they are. That's a lot for a 9-year-old to grab hold of and adopt as a strategy for reaching out for a dream.

I wonder how many times God's "kids" give up on a dream, when He intends so much more for us through creative, outside-the-box thinking? Now, as pastor of one of the fastest growing congregations in America, I get 700 to 1,000 e-mails every week. Many of them are from people wanting to know how to get God's answer to their financial foibles and frustrations.

I received the following e-mail:

> Dear Pastor Bill: I am not really sure what has brought this on, but my husband is at a point where he wants to give up. We have had some financial difficulties, but we could work hard and make them right and he just won't consider that. He says his life is over and he is ready to die. I feel he needs all the help he can get, through prayer, to get God to help him through this most needy time. He is a good man and I just wish we could get on with getting our lives back together and have that good happy life we once had and messed up. We have caused our own problems financially, but I know with the help of God we

can and will get them back together. It just takes time. Frank* feels it is all over permanently and can see no solution. Please help me to pray for him. I love the Lord and I know He wants our lives to work out great, but Frank just doesn't see this. I also know God works best with the power of prayer from many, so I am asking for your advice and prayers before it's too late.

—Melissa*

The end of the money arrives before the end of month in all too many homes. This is not something that just happens when a family with a dad, mom, two kids, a puppy, and minivan comes back from a vacation and finds they simply spent too much on fun and games. It's becoming a daily dilemma, hitting more and more people globally. Single or married, male or female . . . financial stress is no respecter of persons.

What does Scripture say? "Yet have I not seen the righteous forsaken, nor his [God's] seed begging bread" (Psalm 37:25, KJV). Sounds great, but what do I do when I get a notice that says I'm part of the "Workforce Restructuring Program" for my company? That's 21st-century lingo for pink slip. Laid off. Downsized.

I remember when I was just 28 years old and lost my job unexpectedly. I'd done nothing wrong, but my boss had. His errors led to my being unemployed. I had options. I could cry about what I had lost or do something with what I had left. I knew God would provide, but I had to do my part too. I pursued a lead and sure enough it worked out. I was employed again at a local school district. Looking back, I believe my remedy was tied to lifestyle during times of plenty and to the attitude with which I faced my time of job loss. Seed had been sown. My wife and I had always tithed, even when it seemed we could not afford it. Malachi 3:10 says God wants us to test Him in this area of life and see that He will open the windows of heaven to meet our needs. He does not say when He will do it, but He promises to never be late. By the way . . . my boss was my senior pastor. I lost my job because he was ineffective and a church split followed a time of mismanagement of church funds and questionable ministry performance. Financial trials touch the lives of pastors too.

In that same year the church I now pastor was birthed in our living room. A small group of people started meeting and God showed up. It was not long until I lost my job again. This time it was my choice. I had to quit my "day job" to keep up with the demands of pastoring a new church that now has thousands of people in it. But every minute of every day, then and now, has been made possible because of God's faithfulness. He is dependable even when we are not. I have learned about trusting God during times of poverty and plenty.

If you are in the midst of a financial trial, consider the following four steps for financial freedom.

1. Don't give up, look up. Elijah got depressed after fighting the prophets of Baal. He had just won atop Mount Carmel, but somehow he did not think God had enough game left in Him to provide power and grace to contend with Jezebel. God's word to Elijah is the same for you: He's got others in the same situation and they have not given up on God. Don't you give up either! Trust Him!

2. Refuse to be limited to what you are familiar with. I've heard it said, "If you always do what you've always done, you'll always get what you've always got!" What does that suggest? Think outside the box. Bounce your ideas off friends and family. Write things down. Pray. Let God speak His wisdom into your heart. Lack wisdom? James says God will give it to you *if* you ask. Sometimes by speaking to your mind with a Word from His heart to yours. Sometimes by sending someone your way to bring His answer.

You must start expecting God to speak, and then listen for truth that will move you from the fear of failure that so easily paralyzes us in times of trouble. Write it down. Get familiar with the sense of God's remedy. Learn that God has a Plan B ready when your Plan A flops. Then act on faith that is coupled with wisdom. By the way . . . your Plan B is often God's Plan A anyway.

3. Look for creative answers to your dreams that make sense. I'm not telling anyone to cut lunch like I did in fourth grade, but I am saying that there are practical things believers need to learn about money. I think there should be an 11th commandment that says, "Thou shalt not commit indulgence." The lesson of the Dot Com failures of 2001 and the stock market disasters of 2002 is that it is not wise to spend money on things that you really don't need and really won't use. We are much better off planning for rainy days through frugality while blending portfolios in financial tools that have potential for gain. Remember that Jesus Christ said, "To whom much is given much is required," and that a servant who got talents was supposed to multiply them. He never said to stockpile this world's goods and admire how much we have. He said if you are blessed financially to use those resources as a steward, knowing that they are His, not yours, and that you will give an account when you stand before God of how you invested His money in things eternal. He has no problem with your enjoying earthly goods if an eternal perspective drives your every decision. That's the teaching of Paul to Timothy, his son in the faith. "Tell those who are rich in this world not to be proud and not to trust in their money, which will soon be gone. But their trust should be in the living God, who richly gives us all we need for our enjoyment. Tell them to use their money to do good. They should be rich in good works and should give generously to those in need, always being ready to share with others whatever God has given them. By doing this they will be storing up their treasure as a good foundation for the future so that they may take hold of real life (1 Timothy 6:17-19, NLT).

4. Accept God's answers. Sometimes God's way of answering prayer is by saying, "No." We don't like that one, but He is still our Heavenly Parent. That means He knows best and we do not. So when He chooses a plan for us that's different from our design, we must submit and accept the direction He sends by withholding or supplying bounty. Maybe you should not go on that missions trip. Maybe you should take what you would have spent on your own ministry and give it to someone else. Don't be afraid to let God say "No" as a means to answering your prayer for guidance.

Life can change quickly. So can your financial state. Predetermine in your mind that, regardless of your economic status, you will always trust in God and operate your life on biblical principles.

Most people cannot handle success. It is harder for a wealthy person to give 10 percent than it is for a poor man. Yet the wealthy should give much more than 10 percent, for "to whom much is given much is required." All too often people are blessed by God, then change their theology. They believed it was appropriate to give to God when they felt they needed His blessings to survive, but not when they got enough to trust in their riches. Oh, the folly of such thinking.

I have watched selfish visions of grandeur and self-sufficiency ruin families and destroy the divine potential that God has freely bestowed. Never forget the mandate of Matthew 6:33: Seek first the Kingdom and all you need will be added to you. Then lay up treasure in heaven, not on earth. Those principles, when heeded by a follower of Christ, bind one to God's plan to bless and protect the redeemed. Follow those directions and reap the reward of a life of *discipline* and *dreams*. The two really do go together quite well in the economy of heaven.

*Name has been changed

Bill Buchholz is founding pastor of Family Community Church in South San Jose, California. The church, with over 3,500 attendees, has been called the fastest growing church in Silicon Valley for the past two years by the San Jose Mercury News. Buchholz was chairman of the board for South Bay and East Bay Teen Challenge and served on a Mayor's Task Force in the city of San Jose, as well as other boards and committees.

Prior to starting Family Community Church, Buchholz served as associate pastor and school administrator in another San Jose congregation, and worked in property management and as a school instructor. He still holds teaching credentials with the State Department of Education.

Buchholz and his wife, Melody, have one son and two daughters: Ron, Charice, and Anna. They have one grand-daughter.

12

POVERTY

Planting Seeds for a Better Future

GLEN D. COLE

Perhaps you have heard of the man who said to his wife, "I certainly wish you could bake bread the way my mother used to."

His wife replied, "And I sure wish you could make the dough my father used to."

Solomon was rich and very powerful. Through the course of his life he learned some lessons and wrote about them, particularly in the Book of Proverbs. His experiences touch on a variety of subjects, but none as clear as the subject of *poverty*. It seems as though Solomon had pondered on more than one occasion why some people seemed to have enough for life, and why some did not. This chapter is an effort to discover the answer to why some seem to be destined to plenty while others seem condemned to the slums.

In Proverbs 11:24, this man of ancient time makes this declaration: "There is one who scatters, yet increases more;

and there is one who withholds more than is right, But it leads to poverty" (NKJV).

A definition of this interesting view can be found in *The Message* by Eugene Peterson. His rendering of that verse in Proverbs goes like this: "The world of the generous gets larger and larger; the world of the stingy gets smaller and smaller."

Another way of saying it is: "That which is withheld is no real benefit to him; it only increases his want." Which seems to be what the apostle Paul states in 2 Corinthians 9:6, when he points out, "He which soweth sparingly shall reap also sparingly" (KJV). What is it that Solomon and Paul are saying to this, or any generation of people? It is a warning to those who are stingy in nature—those with a Scrooge mentality. There is a universal law that God has established. It is *the law of the seed.* You can plant a single seed and that tiny seed will develop into something much larger. And notably, that which the single seed becomes always bears a multitude of seeds.

My testimony of this truth is the same as Pastor David Williams' of Mount Hope Ministries in Lansing, Michigan. He confirms the validity of the law of the seed with these words: "Some people forget to keep planting. So their harvest isn't what it should be. But I kept planting. And Harvest Time kept coming—quietly, discreetly, without a lot of noise, but it kept coming. So I increased my giving to 15 percent, then 20 percent, then 25 percent, then 30 percent, then 33 percent of my gross income, then more! These are seeds for my future and for my family's future."

Now read again the discovery of Solomon in Proverbs 11:24 from *The Message*: "The world of the generous gets larger and larger; the world of the stingy gets smaller and smaller."

An anonymous story from my files illustrates vividly the way out of the slums into a life of generosity. The opposite of stinginess pays off in more than just money.

A widowed mother had a 7-year-old son, blind most of his life. A young surgeon brought the case to a great and kindly surgeon who thought an operation could restore sight. But there was no money! Still the surgeon was interested in giving sight to the blind boy. In the boy's bed was a small teddy bear. An arm was gone, a leg broken. The boy could not go to sleep without that teddy bear. The operation was success-ful. The boy was able to see his mother for the first time. As he was leaving the hospital, the boy walked up to the great surgeon and said, "Doctor, here is my teddy bear. We can't pay you money, so I'm giving you my teddy bear to pay for my operation."

When the family got home, a huge package was awaiting them. Inside they found the largest and finest teddy bear that money could buy. But in a famous surgeon's office in a large eastern city, carefully placed under glass on top of a beautiful bookcase, triumphantly sat a little brown, battered teddy bear. One arm was gone, a leg was broken, one eye was lost, but that teddy bear's one good eye was shining. On a card just in front of the little bear, the doctor had written: "The largest single fee I have ever received for professional services."

Another observation of Solomon on this subject of poverty comes in Proverbs 28:22: "A man with an evil eye hastens after riches, and does not consider that poverty will come upon him" (NKJV). Mr. Peterson in *The Message* translates this to mean "get-rich-quick schemes are rip-offs." The preacher in this text is implying that a man's grasping greed brings no blessing with it. The Spanish have a proverb based on this verse. It reads: "Who would be rich in a year gets hanged in half a year."

I heard a basketball player from a university say to the press, "My main goal is money!" Poverty comes to the person who has to grasp and "get rich quick." The problem seems to be in not being able to let go. This trend is illustrated in the story of the eagle feeding upon a dead lamb on a large sheet of ice floating down the Niagara when great hunks of ice were breaking loose during the spring thaw. As the floating ice came dangerously near the falls the eagle tried to stretch his wings and fly to safety, but the mist from the river had caused the bird's wings to freeze and its strength was not sufficient to get them loose. Over the brink to its death went the eagle, with a piercing scream that was heard above the roar of the falls.

The third observation of Solomon to be noted is in Proverbs 13:18: "Poverty and shame will come to him who neglects discipline, but he who regards reproof will be honored" (NASV).

This speaks to the one who is "headstrong in pursuing his own plans." Stubbornness can be a sure means of discovering poverty. One man in the Old Testament portrays this so clearly. The stories are found in the Book of Judges. In chapter 14, Samson is arguing with his parents about his desire to take a wife from among the Philistines. He becomes very stubborn and refuses their advice. The wife acquired by his stubbornness ends up being burned with her father by the Philistines. Chapter 16 contains the story of Delilah, the next woman in Samson's life. She entices him until he reveals the secret of his strength. Both of them die with the Philistines as he pulls down the pillars of the temple.

Doing what you want to do instead of what you should do can lead to poverty and shame.

Proverbs 20:13 speaks to a malady that many seem to possess in this life: "Do not love sleep, lest you come to poverty" (NKJV). That is a warning against laziness. I read a statement years ago that has never left my mind. "The lazier a man is, the more he intends to do tomorrow." The second part of the verse just quoted says this: "Open your eyes, and you will be satisfied with bread." This refers to getting up in the morning and using one's time to profitable advantage. All of us have the same amount of time each day. No one has more or less than the other. Each of us gets 24 hours, each of us has 60 minutes per hour, and each has to deal with 60 seconds per minute. The president of the United States has no more time than you or I have. Keeping out of poverty depends on how we use what has been given us. Laziness will lead to poverty.

Another statement by King Solomon is in Proverbs 23:21 where he deals with feeding the flesh: "For the drunkard and the glutton will come to poverty, and drowsiness will clothe a man with rags." The habits of self-indulgence undermine the strength of the body and the vigor of the mind until poverty comes like an armed man. Esau was never the same after coming in from the field and smelling the stew his brother was cooking up on the family stove. Esau said, "Feed me." You perhaps remember Jacob's reply, "Sell me your birthright as of this day." Amazingly, that is exactly what Esau did. So "Jacob gave Esau bread and stew of lentils; then he ate and drank, arose, and went his way" (Genesis 25:34).

It is difficult to "bear in our body the marks of the Lord Jesus" (Galatians 6:17). The challenge to a generation that has so much is found in Paul's words to the Galatian believers, "Those who are Christ's have crucified the flesh with its passions and desires" (Galatians 5:24). Watch out for the poverty brought about by feeding the flesh.

Our last observation is from Proverbs 28:18 where Scripture reminds us, "Whoever walks blamelessly will be saved, but he who is perverse in his ways will suddenly fall." An alternate rendering is, "Walk straight—live well and be saved; a devious life is a doomed life" (*The Message*).

This word "devious" refers to "craftiness." It speaks of the skillful deceiving of others. Two other words apply here. They are "sly" and "tricky." Poverty comes to those who fall into this lifestyle. We deal with people even in ministry who vacillate between right and wrong. Even leaders can pretend to be pursuing one path while really taking another. They "will fall suddenly."

Jacob made an effort to disguise himself as Esau before his father. He said, "I am Esau your firstborn" (Genesis 27:19). Years later Jacob met Laban, the father of Rachel. He found this man to be even craftier than himself. The warning of Numbers 32:23 is this: "Be sure your sin will find you out."

The same man who gave us the Proverbs observations writes what he calls the "conclusion of the whole matter" in Ecclesiastes 12:13: "Fear God, and keep his commandments: for this is the whole duty of man. For God shall bring every work into judgment, with every secret thing, whether it be good, or whether it be evil" (KJV).

God is good to every one of us. He has blessed us with so many things on this earth. We ought to say, "Dear Lord, because of Your goodness to me, I know that I ought to give my best to You." God has supplied us with everything we have. Are we going to soak it all up like a sponge and give nothing in return for all of His blessings? I hope not! Let us continually be planting seed so that God can grow us into plants of productivity and blessing to others. He wants to keep us from the poverty of slum-like living!

Glen D. Cole serves as district superintendent of the Northern California and Nevada District Council of the Assemblies of God. Dr. Cole served some 17 years as senior pastor of Capital Christian Center in Sacramento, California, a 4,000-member congregation. He served on the Executive Presbytery of the General Council of the Assemblies of God for 10 years. He has been a member of the Foreign Missions Board and has served as the chairman of the Board of Directors for Central Bible College in Springfield, Missouri. He has ministered throughout the world at numerous conferences, district councils, camp meetings, and churches. He has authored or coauthored numerous books and articles. A graduate of Central Bible College in Springfield, Missouri, he was awarded a doctor of divinity degree from Pacific Coast Bible College in Sacramento. He and his wife, Mary Ann, have two sons, who are also ministers, and seven grandchildren.

13

TRAGEDY

Stages of Recovery

JIMMIE D. BREWER

The day begins like any other, but before it is over we learn that all of our 10 children and their homes have been destroyed, along with most of our material possessions. To complicate matters, in the days following we suffer devastating personal physical sickness. While this may seem like an improbable and unrealistic scenario, this story was real for a man whose experiences are recorded in the Book of Job.

Job has served for years as a classic example for individuals who are suffering. However, in this chapter, we will examine Job as he goes through the five stages of grief—denial, anger, bargaining, depression, and acceptance.[1] This five-staged process which we can observe in the Book of Job is a normal process that individuals—even today—go through following a tragedy.[2] In my years of counseling, I have observed that individuals who, by God's grace, are able to understand and work through these five stages successfully have a greater probability of long-term, healthy emotional recovery from a traumatic event.

DENIAL

The first stage a person experiences following the shock of a trauma is *denial*. Immediately after his ordeal, Job seems to be unaffected by the whole matter (Job 1:20 through 2:10, NIV). He was very philosophical about the whole series of tragic events when he stated to his wife, "Naked I came from my mother's womb, and naked I will depart. The LORD gave and the LORD has taken away" (1:21). He said nothing foolish, and seemed to take everything that had happened to him in stride.

When problems overwhelm us, normally our first reaction is to deny the reality of how bad things are. If you doubt this, just remember on Tuesday morning, September 11, 2001, how you were thinking as you watched the World Trade Center on fire. I was thinking, *They will get the fires put out soon, and everything will be okay and back to normal.* Our minds and emotions have a difficult time dealing with tragedy and events of this magnitude. That is OK! For that is the way God made us—and it is only step one in the recovery process.

ANGER

The second stage is *anger*.[3] While Job is able to say the right things in the early days of his loss, deep within him there is tremendous hurt and anguish. In chapter 3 it all begins to pour out when he opens his speech by cursing the day of his birth. The anger within him bursts when he states,

"I have no peace, no quietness; I have no rest, but only turmoil" (3:26). When the reality of our problems starts to sink in, the underlying deep emotional responses begin to spill out, and in our anger we question why this has happened to us. Our anger can go in many directions and have many targets. We can even become angry at God. To suppress our emotions at this time and turn our anger inward only causes bitterness. To turn our anger outward can result in improper behavior. It is important to recognize and understand our anger and deal with it appropriately with the help of a confidant or a Christian counselor so that this emotion of anger can be channeled into a constructive direction. God provided this stage to awaken the *fight* within us to help us to recover and survive. For many it is the first time that they begin to care about going on with their lives since the tragedy. Without this stage, we could literally grieve ourselves to death.

BARGAINING

If the anger is addressed, we then can begin to feel a need to take charge of our lives. It is at this point that *bargaining* begins (cf. 9:29-35 and 23:1-7). Job cries out for *his day in court.* He first pleads for an arbitrator to present his case, and then he expresses his confidence to present his own defense. He believes that if he could only present his case, God would deliver him from the pain of his ordeal. Bargaining comes in many forms. For some it may be trying to *make a deal* with God. It may be sacrificing or trying to be more *spiritual* to influence God to provide a *short cut* through the pain. Others may go through this bargaining stage in an attempt to find solutions to the pain they are experiencing following a tragedy. But all bargaining at its core is feeling that we can do something to get God to change the course of events in our lives—or that we can and should be able to *fix* the problem ourselves. Understanding that these bargaining emotions are normal will help us to be patient as we journey through this stage. It is God's way of helping us understand the limits of our own power and capabilities. But remember, God's grace and love do not change—even while we are bargaining or trying to fix it ourselves!

DEPRESSION

Finally, exhaustion sets in as the emotional stress takes its toll and we begin to experience *depression*. We are just too tired to struggle anymore. Nothing we have tried in our human endeavors through the earlier stages has relieved our anguish. Every emotional anchor we thought we had has let go, and our hope for solutions turns to hopelessness as our struggle becomes silent. There is no need to talk or try anymore. For Job this silence comes in the middle of God's message to him (cf. 40:1-5). He understands he has no solutions, and he has not fully realized the sovereignty of God in the whole matter. Part of our healthy recovery is to *give up* and come to a point when we are out of answers and solutions. This is God's way of preparing us for the final stage of healthy emotional recovery—in His time.

ACCEPTANCE

At the end of this grief cycle Job is able to discover *acceptance* (cf. 42:1-6). He still does not know why the tragedy has happened, but that no longer matters. For God has broken through Job's human limitations. He will no longer question God. He finally comes to terms with what has happened. He enters into a warm, trusting relationship with God. The *war* is over, and now a much more mature Job finds the God of his past—for the first time—again! Job can now live his life with integrity and wholeness (cf. 42:7-17). The last stage in a healthy emotional recovery is accepting what has happened to us without the debilitating effects of regret. We now can embrace the next phase of our journey of life with the knowledge that we have not cut short the process. We have allowed God by His grace to take a negative situation and bring us through the appropriate stages. And in doing so, He has developed us into stronger and wiser children of God—ready to move on with the rest of our lives having a greater appreciation for the wisdom and sovereignty of God.

THE RECOVERY PROCESS

There are some basic principles that each person needs to follow during the process of recovery as outlined in this chapter. They are as follows:

1. The length of time for the full grief cycle will vary depending on the personality of each individual, the depth of tragedy, and one's circumstances. It may take some people up to two years or longer to recover.

2. Major life decisions made before the grief cycle is completed are often regretted later. This is because we are changing so much during the grief cycle (especially when the grief is the loss of a spouse or close loved one). When the grief cycle is over and we are ready to move on, we normally will look at the world very differently.

3. To rush the process can create an artificial sense of being through the cycle. When this is done, additional emotional problems may develop.

4. Because of the emotional and physical stress and exhaustion we experience as a result of the recovery process, trusting ourselves to know when we are through the grief cycle is not always advisable. Therefore, it is very important that we have trusted and competent individuals in our lives who can be honest with us and help us to know when, in fact, we have reached the acceptance stage.

5. As Christians we can ask God to help us be patient and give us strength through the process. We should also realize that God has not left us, but through His sovereignty and grace He is guiding us through the stages of recovery (cf. Romans 8:28-39).

6. While the stages in this chapter have been presented in an even and sequential manner, real life does not always work this neatly. Our individual journey through these stages may be uneven, and we may even go back to previous stages. The important thing is that we continue to let the process work until we reach the final stage of acceptance.

It is God's desire to bring us *through* the grief cycle, but He wants to do so on His terms and in His time. It is not that He desires for us to suffer more—but that we learn to trust Him in another area of our lives. Job finally did get an answer to his question, "Why do the righteous suffer?"

God's answer: "Trust Me."

But it was only on the other side of the grief cycle that Job could *accept* that answer and move on with his life—a stronger and wiser person.

Jimmie D. Brewer is director of church leadership and professor of pastoral communication and administration at Bethany College of the Assemblies of God, where he has served since 1991. An ordained minister with the Assemblies of God, he is also senior pastor of Aptos Christian Fellowship in Aptos, California (since 1996). Both his father and mother were credentialed ministers with the Assemblies of God.

Brewer holds a D.Min. from Harding University Graduate School of Religion, an M.Div. and an M.A. in Biblical Studies from Assemblies of God Theological Seminary and a B.S. in Business Administration from Arkansas State University.

He has served as vice president for academics at Bethany, and as academic dean and director of continuing education at Southwestern Assemblies of God University in Waxahachie, Texas. He has also taught and coached in the Missouri Public School system. He served four other senior pastorates—in Advance, Missouri; Booneville, Arkansas; Senath, Missouri; and Cardwell, Missouri.

Brewer has served on various district and national committees and has been a seminar speaker and written articles for several publications.

Brewer and his wife, Peggy, are the parents of two, LaDonna and David. They have three grandchildren.

14

DEATH

Our Journey Through a Dark Time

PAUL VELIQUETTE

"I will give you the treasures of darkness,
riches stored in secret places,
so that you may know that I am the LORD,
the God of Israel, who calls you by name."
(Isaiah 45:3, NIV)

THE ANNOUNCEMENT

Come with me on a journey through one of my family's most difficult times. Glenda and I were thrilled by the prospect of becoming grandparents for the first time. As the grandpa-to-be, I prepared a special PowerPoint presentation with pictures of Jennifer (our daughter) and Gareth (our son-in-law) as toddlers and a humorous pose of uncle-to-be Jason. Our son, Jason, who was doing a ministerial internship at Timberline Church in Fort Collins, Colorado, had arranged to be with us that Sunday. Because of the family atmosphere at Abundant Life, it was an appropriate moment for us to celebrate the birth of a child to our youth pastors, Gareth and Jennifer. The joy of the moment was indescribable. We eagerly looked forward to the birth of this child. I was now a proud grandfather!

THE TELEPHONE CALL

Less than two weeks later, I got the call on my cell phone from Jennifer. With a voice choked with emotion, she said, "Dad, we got really bad news today. They could not find our baby's heartbeat."

Our baby—theirs, ours, the church's—was dead. I immediately pulled over to the side of the road. I can only begin to describe the unbelievable feeling that came over me. It was as if I was in a deep, dark hole, and the sides were caving in on me. An emotional explosion took place in my heart and mind. It was a time of uncontrolled feelings of despair, anger, extreme sadness, and helplessness. Not only was I hurting, but my "little girl" was in extreme pain. Nothing is harder on a dad than the pain of his child. This was our daughter's second loss of an unborn child in a year. The only thing I could say in that moment was, "I love you, Jen. We are coming over."

THE ROOM

As we walked into the room, there was a strange mixture of increased sorrow yet a sense of safety. We were now together as family—loving, caring, embracing, weeping, whispering words of love and support. We sat mostly in silence, each deep in our own thoughts and emotions, each attempting to find a steady place to stand. The verse came to mind where Paul says about the body of Christ, "If one part suffers, every part suffers with it" (1 Corinthians 12:26). We were hurting, confused, and dazed.

THE SECOND ANNOUNCEMENT

I normally look forward to Sunday morning with great joy and anticipation. The following Sunday was not such a day. We had cried a lot that week. Was there any emotion left? How could I have the strength to even stand before our church family? "Lord, why is this happening? Why the public announcement just two weeks ago and now this?" I did not feel like a tower of strength. I did not want to be there. But God is faithful.

Early in the morning before the sun came up, the Word came. The Word, God's very own words, came resounding into my heart. Words I had stored up in my heart now came forward. Words that now had deeper meaning and significance. Words read a thousand times become meaningful because they speak to you in a moment of your life. It was the words of Paul from his letter to the Corinthian church: "We are hard pressed on every side, but not crushed; perplexed, but not in despair; persecuted, but not abandoned; struck down, but not destroyed" (2 Corinthians 4:8). The meaning began to slowly impact my mind and heart. It was like a big ocean liner that takes time to gain speed and momentum because of its size.

Yes, God, I think I am getting it. We are hard pressed, we are perplexed, we are struck down. Yes, this death has caused us to feel like we are hard pressed. We have been perplexed; we have asked a lot of questions; we have been angry with You, God! It has been a terrible blow! We had prayed for a child. Jennifer and Gareth rearranged their lives in preparation for the birth of this child. It has knocked us down. We hear the referee calling out the count: one, two, three, four, five, six, seven, eight, nine.... But wait, the count is halted. God, You say pressed but not crushed, perplexed but not in despair! Is it true? Can it be true? How can we make it true?

It was as if I were getting a spiritual transfusion from the Word of God. The anemia of my spirit was being replaced with the potency of His precious Word. That was it! It was a faith thing! It is believing without understanding; it is knowing without evidence; it is trusting Him because He is the I Am.

I approached the podium slowly that morning with my Bible opened to that passage. Slowly and deliberately, I read, "We are hard pressed." I read it twice. Then I read it on the personal level. "I am hard pressed, I am perplexed, I am struck down."

God was there. His Holy Spirit was there. The meaning of our church's vision statement now came true on a personal level. Abundant Life Christian Center is a vibrant *haven*. The Church, the body of Christ, provides safety.

That was the beginning of the process that still continues in our healing and restoration. We have discovered God's *treasures of darkness* referred to in Isaiah 45:3.

TREASURE #1

We are created by God as emotional people.

It is not just OK to feel emotions; it is essential to feel and express emotions when you lose an unborn child. Just because you have not seen the child does not mean that it is not a tremendous loss. It is death. Therefore, you will and must mourn. Yes, we know that God is in control. Yes, we know that "all things work together for good." You will get there in your journey of recovery.

The first step is expressing all of your emotions, even the ones you may not consider "Christian." Do what you need to do. Some weep; some holler at God; some are quiet; some huddle up with close friends; some want to be alone. God has wired each of us differently and uniquely. Find your way and just do it. Our family discovered that tolerance and acceptance of each other's emotional makeup was essential for healthy grieving.

TREASURE #2

Bad things happen to good people.

This age-old question will resurface on a personal level if you lose your child. "Why us?" Jennifer and Gareth did it right; they did it in God's order—marriage first and then a baby. They had taken all the steps to be financially and emotionally ready for a child. Yes, God does often provide special protection for His children. I loved hearing the stories of how Christian people were spared in the World Trade Center on 9/11. However, some awesome, devoted followers of Christ lost their lives on that day.

This world is broken. Sin broke this world. It cannot be fixed. It is so far beyond repair that God will someday create a new heaven and a new earth. Until that time, we live in a messed up, confusing, bewildering world where bad things happen to good people.

TREASURE #3

You are not alone.

There is good news. You are not alone. As followers of Christ, we have been blessed by this special community called the family of God. Not only do you have your immediate, physical family, but you have this huge, wonderful, diverse, helping, caring, burden-lifting community of faith. We could not have done it without that family. The Bible says, "A new commandment I give you: Love one another. As I have loved you, so you must love one another. All men will know that you are my disciples if you love one another" (John 13:34). Let the community of faith know you hurt. Yes, it is awkward and uncomfortable. People do not always know what to say. You will not always know how to respond. Do it anyway.

TREASURE #4

Find a few close friends to gather around you.

None of us has the emotional strength to share the details of our hurts with a large group of people. You come to a point where you don't want to say another word to anyone. You are tempted to prepare a handout that just says, "Here, this is what is happening and how I feel." Find one or two people who are your closest friends to support you. They can share information with the rest of the community of faith about your situation. I have friends like this. Bob Cook, among others, is such a friend who shared with me my sorrow and pain. He wept with me and helped to lift a burden too heavy to carry on my own. Glenda, my wife, found *riches stored in secret places* from her accountability group with Lynn Ruby and Marnie Allen, friends who allow her to experience waves of grief as she did at a baby dedication. It made a difference.

TREASURE #5

Let there be deep healing.

Some time ago, I had an accident in a chemistry lab and spilled concentrated nitric acid on myself. The instructor immediately poured a neutralizing solution on my burns. However, he missed a spot on my leg, which caused a deep acid burn. Because of the depth of the burn, the doctors would not allow the skin to heal over the wound. They kept the wound open and continued to cleanse the wound so that it would heal from the bottom up. If the skin had grown over the wound, it would have abscessed, which could have caused me to lose my leg. *Let the wound heal from the bottom up.* Don't hurry the process.

TREASURE #6

There is a difference between a wound and a scar.

There will come a time when you are no longer wounded by the loss of your unborn child. Your wound will turn into a scar. Wounds go away. The pain, suffering, and numbness will some day leave you. For some it may be a quick process. For others it will take some time. You must do things that will facilitate healing. Be in church, spend time in prayer and in the Bible. But most importantly, do not put fun on hold! Do fun things; be with fun people. Laugh until you hurt! It will heal. The scar, however, will remain.

There will always be reminders. Scars can continue to be sensitive to touch. People will see the scars and ask questions. It will be okay. God will then help you help others. You will be able to say with Paul, "Praise be to the God and Father of our Lord Jesus Christ, the Father of compassion and the God of all comfort, who comforts us in all our troubles, so that we can comfort those in any trouble with the comfort we ourselves have received from God" (2 Corinthians 1:3,4).

TREASURE #7

God still loves you.

Losing an unborn child is not punishment from God. This has not happened because He no longer loves you. He will show His love to you as you walk this journey of sorrow. Psalm 23:4 says, "Even though I walk through the valley of the shadow of death, I will fear no evil, for you are with me." Never forget that Jesus walked the path of death himself. It was a path of sorrow, a journey of grief, a life- giving, death-requiring journey. It was up the hill called The Skull.

He knows your pain. He understands death, sorrow, and mourning. He is with you! I know. I am there, and He is with me.

Paul Veliquette is senior pastor of Abundant Life Christian Center in Arvada, Colorado, where he has served since 1988 (since 1992 as senior pastor; prior to that as executive pastor). He serves as presbyter for the North Denver Metro Section of the Rocky Mountain District of the Assemblies of God. He served at Craig Memorial Chapel in Scotts Valley, California, from 1971-1981 as minister of youth and Christian education during two interim periods.

Veliquette and his wife, Glenda, have three children: Jennifer (Veliquette) Unruh, Jason Veliquette, and Gareth Unruh (son-in-law).

15

BETRAYAL

Overcoming Disloyalty and Distrust

ERIC HANSEN

The pain is as real as though they had pressed a hot iron to your flesh. Initially there was shock and hurt, but then came the blisters of bitterness and ultimate brokenness. How could this person whom you loved and trusted so much use such a sharp sword on you when in the not-so-distant past it was used to defend you?

How could they do that to you? He or she was your friend, a confidant, someone you had trusted to watch your back. Then one day, unexpectedly, unrepentantly, the person hurt you so deeply that you're not sure if you will ever completely heal from such a deep wound.

IT'S HAPPENED BEFORE

Do you remember the man in the Bible named Malchus? He was the man who, on the night Jesus was betrayed, had his ear cut off by Peter. To refresh your memory read this passage from the Gospel of John closely and note *who* it was who swung the sword.

> When he had finished praying, Jesus left with his disciples and crossed the Kidron Valley. On the other side there was an olive grove, and he and his disciples went into it.
>
> Now Judas, who betrayed him, knew the place, because Jesus had often met there with his disciples. So Judas came to the grove, guiding a detachment of soldiers and some officials from the chief priests and Pharisees. They were carrying torches, lanterns and weapons.
>
> Jesus, knowing all that was going to happen to him, went out and asked them, "Who is it you want?"
>
> "Jesus of Nazareth," they replied.
>
> "I am he," Jesus said. (And Judas the traitor was standing there with them.) When Jesus said, "I am he," they drew back and fell to the ground.
>
> Again he asked them, "Who is it you want?"
>
> And they said, "Jesus of Nazareth."
>
> "I told you that I am he," Jesus answered. "If you are looking for me, then let these men go." This happened so that the words he had spoken would be fulfilled: "I have not lost one of those you gave me."
>
> Then Simon Peter, who had a sword, drew it and struck the high priest's servant, cutting off his right ear. (The servant's name was Malchus.)
>
> (John 18:1-10, NIV)

The parallel passage of this account in Luke ends in chapter 22 verse 51 as Jesus picks up the bloodied and severed ear, and reattaches it to bring a total healing to Malchus.

SO WHAT DOES THAT HAVE TO DO WITH ME?

Peter, the man who wielded the sword and caused such a grievous injury, was a follower of Jesus. He was a radical Christian. He loved the Lord and was even willing to fight for what he believed in and to protect his Savior. However, in his zealousness he drew his sword—all the while believing he was doing the Lord a favor—and struck a servant of the high priest, leaving his bloodied ear lying in the dust. Most likely Peter was not aiming for Malchus' ear. He had probably taken direct aim at the young servant's throat, only to miss and hit his ear as the young man ducked out of the way.

COULD IT BE?

Could it be that the person who struck the blow to your life was also thinking they were doing the Lord a favor? Could it be that they were actually aiming for your throat and not your ear? Could it be that they were being zealous for the things of God but acting out their zeal in the wrong way? Could it be that they had really intended to "kill" you but by the grace of God they only hit your "ear"?

THERE IS HEALING

Malchus, I'm sure, was amazed as the Lord reached down and picked up his once-attached ear, then, with a single movement, stretched out His hand and put it back in place, perfectly. It was amazing, miraculous, something that only Jesus could do. A story that, should Malchus later that evening recount it to Mrs. Malchus, she too would find hard to believe. There was not even a scar!

DON'T TOUCH THAT EAR!

Don't you find Malchus' reaction interesting? When Jesus reached out to reattach it, Malchus did not pull back and say, "No!" He could have said, "Jesus, don't touch that ear, it's mine! I want to keep it in a special box so that when others ask me about my injury I can then take it out of the box and show everyone what a Christian by the name of Peter did to me." If that were the case, I'm sure Malchus would have gotten all sorts of attention and sympathy for years to come.

Often, after you've been injured, even by a fellow Christian, you might be tempted to hold onto the memory of that assault and keep it in a "box." But, friend, when you do that you are refusing the healing touch of the Master.

I KNOW IT'S NOT EASY

No one ever said that being a Christian would be easy. It's bad enough that evil people want to hurt, betray, and ruin what fragile trust there might be in a relationship. But how much deeper the cut when a trusted Christian friend takes a swing at your neck? The wound is real. The cut is deep. And the devil doesn't want you whole. He wants to rub salt in that open wound. He would love to see the injury get infected with bitterness and a bad attitude that will eventually spread to your friends and family.

GET YOUR PRAISE ON

I speak from experience—as someone who has experienced the nearly deadly blow of betrayal and the firsthand fallout of distrust. If you let the devil get a foothold on your attitude, he will eventually turn it into a choke hold. So whether your death is by strangulation or a vicious cut of a friend, Satan could really care less. The end result is still the same—your death. Your death is his goal. Don't let him score!

You might be asking yourself, "Did this persecution, this affliction, this near-fatal wound come from God as a wake-up call for me? Did it come because I was oblivious, too engrossed in my life and God needed to get my attention? Is the origin of my trouble God or Satan?"

Here is what I've learned.

If it is a test from God:

Praise the Lord as it says to do in Psalm 150. To praise the Lord while in your trial shows the Father the attitude of your heart. It demonstrates to Him that your heart is pure, your hands are clean and your motives are uncontaminated. This must always be your reaction when tests come your way.

If the blow is from Satan:

To praise the Lord in the face of Satan is to remind him of his ultimate demise. "Now thanks be unto God, which always causeth us to triumph in Christ" (2 Corinthians 2:14, KJV).

So whatever the source of your conflict, the answer that always wins the Lord's favor is to "get your praise on!"

Job said it this way: "Though he slay me, yet will I trust in him" (Job 13:15). Remember this simple piece of theology that will carry you through a lifetime: "God good; devil bad."

GOD IS GOOD

As time goes by and you make a conscious effort to put the healing "balm in Gilead" on your wound, I believe you'll be able to say as Joseph did to his murderous brothers, "You intended to harm me, but God intended it for good to accomplish what is now being done, the saving of many lives" (Genesis 50:20, NIV). God is good and wants to use you and this horrible incident in your life to teach, train, and help others through similar circumstances. Jesus wants to pick up that severed ear and reattach it. Will you let Him? Will you allow Him to heal your hurt?

NO MORE SCAR

It is now the midnight hour in the spring of the year while the dirt along the narrow path is still damp with the evening's dew. The betrayer comes with a dishonest kiss that identifies Jesus as the One to be arrested. In a swirl of burning torches, there is chaos: shouts, anger, pushing and shoving, until the inevitable happens. A sword is drawn. Not the sword of a heathen, but of Peter, a man of God. A man who thought he was doing the Lord's will. Then, after his moment of anger, there on the damp ground lay Malchus' ear. The crowd goes silent. What will the Master say? But not speaking a word, Jesus bent down, picked up the ear and healed Malchus. Not using a bandage, stitches, gauze or tape, Jesus healed him completely.

HOW ABOUT YOU?

Will you let this deep cut become infected and ultimately bring your death? Or will you praise God through this trial and come out the other side not even smelling of smoke? "So Shadrach, Meshach and Abednego came out of the fire, and the satraps, prefects, governors and royal advisers crowded around them. They saw that the fire had not harmed their bodies, nor was a hair of their heads singed; their robes were not scorched, and there was no smell of fire on them" (Daniel 3:26,27).

You have been created by God for greatness. You have a purpose and a grand destiny in life. Determine right now that no devil in hell will keep you from hitting your mark. You are more than a conqueror! Right now pray this prayer out loud and let the Lord heal your hurt and set you free:

"Father, I forgive _____ (insert that person's name) for what they did to me. I release them from my thoughts of anger and revenge. Today, I choose to praise You, even in my trial. I release my bad attitudes and ask that You would heal my heart from this horrible hurt and not even leave a scar. I need You, Jesus, to touch this wound, to bring relief and cause me to triumph as Your Word has promised. I now leave this person and this situation here with You, at the foot of the cross. 'I [choose to] press on to take hold of that for which Christ Jesus took hold of me. . . . [I now forget] what is behind and [strain] toward what is ahead. I press on toward the goal to win the prize for which God has called me heavenward in Christ Jesus' (Philippians 3:12-14, NIV). In Jesus' name, Amen."

Eric A. Hansen is the senior pastor of First Assembly of God in Springfield, Illinois. The church operates as a "Government of 12" cell-based church, releasing leaders into the harvestfield. During Hansen's tenure, the original 100-member church has outgrown the current facility, purchased 30 acres of land on Interstate 55, and has plans to build a state-of-the-art facility to seat 2,200 people. Hansen and his associate pastor wife, Cheryl, have one daughter, Hannah Jean. Hansen is a graduate of North Central University of the Assemblies of God (B.A.) and Evangel Christian University (Th.M.).

16

MIDLIFE CRISIS

Overcoming the Deception of Lack

DAVID CRISPIN

"And you are complete through your union with Christ" (Colossians 2:10, NLT).

Watch television, and get bombarded with a barrage of commercials and appeals, all of which use state-of-the-art graphics, cutting-edge creativity and the latest marketing analysis. Turn on the computer and get shelled with a series of pop-up commercial applets that hit your screen in rapid fire, leaving you to fight them off like they were a swarm of territorial bees assailing an intruder. Visit the mailbox and shuffle through piles of unwanted solicitation, last-chance appeals and once-in-a-lifetime promotions. Dare I even mention the phone calls, magazines, papers, the knock on the door—all of which are simply a part of a high-tech, high-stakes, hard-sell game of psychological warfare to get the consumer to experience a sense of lack? Economics thrive on it, government is financed by it, and livelihoods are made from it. Let's face it, advertising works—primarily because it touts the notion that we are incomplete without a certain product. It produces anxiety.

The enemy, unfortunately, also understands the power that lack has on us. The destructive cycle that ensues as a result of lack or incompleteness can cause churches to fall into error, finances to shatter, marriages to dissolve, innocence to be lost, reputations to be soiled, and lives destroyed. Contentment and completeness are found in Christ, but be warned—it can be bad for economics, and harsh on affairs, vices and fads.

THE SUGGESTION OF LACK

Satan suggested to Eve that she was incomplete, not knowing good and evil. It does not seem that there was much of a struggle. Once the deception of lack was entertained by Eve, anxiety was not far behind. Salesmen understand that the sale informally closes once the customer gives in to the anxiety created by lack. In Eve's case, anxiety led to experimentation and Satan watched this destructive cycle bring down "God's image" in the earth.

God knew that this disobedience involved someone's speaking this lack into her life. "Who told you that you were naked?" (Genesis 3:11). Satan's own sense of lack, which led to a rebellion against God, was now being spoken to Eve.

The Bible warns us to be careful whom we listen to, because an attitude of lack can be transferred. First Corinthians 15:33 says, "Bad company corrupts good character." God warns young men that the "lips of an immoral woman drip honey, And her mouth is smoother than oil" (Proverbs 5:3, NKJV). Temptation relies on a sense of lack in order to work.

Israel accepted the lie that they were incomplete and disadvantaged because they did not have a king. They wanted to be like other nations. Acting on this sense of lack, their anxiety-filled response was, "But we will have a king over us, that we also may be like all the nations, and that our king may judge us and go out before us and fight our battles" (1 Samuel 8:19b,20). Despite warnings, their minds were made up. God's leadership was not enough. A sense of lack put this nation on a destructive track.

The churches of Galatia erred in departing from true theology, suggesting that justification by the works of the Law was superior to justification by grace and faith. The Galatians were anxious to go back under the Law. Paul knew that someone had to speak out about this position. "Who has bewitched you that you should not obey the truth?" (Galatians 3:1a). The voices of lack are dangerous voices.

"Midlife crisis" is a time when men deal with the deception of lack. Anxiety makes it worse, because it can lead to experimentation. Is your job enough? Is your marriage enough? Is your image, your life enough? Is God enough? And like the commercials, the applets, and the endless solicitations, a number of quick-fix opportunities parade by you at a time when the suggestion of lack is the strongest. The deception of lack will always demand a sacrifice. Satan uses something we all have—basic needs—and perverts them beyond reason. Example: He tries to convince us to live to eat, instead of eat to live. The same principle applies to sex, money . . . anything.

Giving in to lack is not like taking a test drive in a new car. Take it around the block, adjust the seats, check out the stereo, slip quickly through the gears, smile at the zero to 60 mph time, then come to your senses, take an aspirin for the fever, and toss the keys back to a disappointed salesman. Lack will not let you off that easily. Once the destructive cycle hits the experimental stage, a sacrifice will be made. You just bought the car. When we buy into the proverbial "grass is greener on the other side" mind-set, we waste valuable God-given resources and energies through experimentation and wondering.

Adam and Eve knew it the moment their eyes were opened and they realized that they were naked. Instead of fulfillment, they found themselves lonely, confused, and lost. Their sacrifice was great. The deception of lack took a terrible toll on their lives. Lost intimacy and fellowship with God left Adam and Eve to deal with the numbing reality that the cost would far exceed any benefit.

Israel did not get what they hoped for. The addition of a king only brought more war, more exploitation, and flawed, unstable leadership. This quick fix sacrificed God-inspired leadership for a self-serving leadership and rapidly turned into a nightmare.

Paul the apostle carefully outlined the sacrifice that the churches of the Galatians would make. This sense of lack and incompleteness would cost them the "blessing" and put them under a "curse" (Galatians 3:10). It would cost them the promise and position of sonship and make them slaves again (Galatians 4:1-7). It would cost them their liberty and take them back into bondage (Galatians 5:1-6). It would cost them peace and mercy and bring them back into fear (implied in Galatians 6:16). No wonder Paul said, "You have fallen from [God's] grace" (Galatians 5:4). Grace was sacrificed. Thus Paul inquired, "Who hindered you from obeying the truth?"

(Galatians 5:7). Paul challenged the notion that salvation could be acquired by "keeping the law."

Proverbs chapter five seems to be written just for men who face that long dark night of the soul called midlife crisis. God warns that any sacrifice to fill this sense of lack will be great. "If you do, you will lose your honor and hand over to merciless people everything you have achieved in life. Strangers will obtain your wealth, and someone else will enjoy the fruit of your labor. Afterward you will groan in anguish when disease consumes your body" (Proverbs 5:9-11, NLT). "I have come to the brink of utter ruin, and now I must face public disgrace" (Proverbs 5:14). Fires begin to go out in relationships when the energy necessary to keep the relationship alive is spent "drinking from another well" (Proverbs 5:15). Disastrous consequences ensue, not the least of which is that our own "well" becomes vulnerable to outside temptation. Proverbs 27:7 says, "Honey seems tasteless to a person who is full, but even bitter food tastes sweet to the hungry."

The good news is the Bible has a God-honoring solution to the deception of lack. Let's look at three key encounters.

1. TRUTH ENCOUNTER

Satan presented suggestions of lack to Christ. "All these things I will give You if You will fall down and worship me" (Matthew 4:9, NKJV). His suggestion was that Christ was incomplete without the glory and power of the earthly kingdoms. This deception would be defeated by a truth encounter. "It is written, 'You shall worship the Lord your God, and Him only you shall serve'" (Matthew 4:10). Jesus said, "And you shall know the truth, and the truth shall make you free" (John 8:32). An encounter with truth overcomes suggestions of lack. Adam and Eve rejected the truth and grabbed the fruit because they lost confidence in God. Israel rejected the truth and clambered for a king because of a lack of confidence in God's judges. The Galatians rejected the truth and reached for the Law because of a lack of faith in grace. Truth defeats the anxiety brought on by the suggestion of lack. Paul said in Colossians 2:9,10, "In Him dwells all the fullness of the Godhead bodily, and you are complete in Him." This truth encounter forms the basis for a "life of contentment." Faith in that truth frees us from the emotion and experimentation that come from lack.

2. POWER ENCOUNTER

Challenging the strongholds and suggestions of the enemy is the next step. It is clear from Scripture that changing mind-sets is a form of spiritual warfare. Second Corinthians 10:4,5 says, "We use God's mighty weapons, not mere worldly weapons, to knock down the Devil's strongholds. With these weapons we break down every proud argument that keeps people from knowing God. With these weapons we conquer their rebellious ideas, and we teach them to obey Christ" (NLT). Paul taught the Romans that they could change their lives by changing the way they think (Romans 12:1,2). This power encounter declares war on the deception of lack. Jesus said, "Get behind me, Satan" (Matthew 16:23). For the man in a midlife crisis, the suggestion must be rejected. Spiritual warfare must come against that suggestion that the wife of one's youth is not enough. Solomon, seeing the devastation in his father's house, declared that men should find content-ment and satisfaction with the "wife of your youth." We must challenge any thought that what God gave us is not enough. Prayer is an effective power encounter. "Watch and pray, that ye enter not into temptation" (Matthew 26:41, KJV). Prayer steers us in the right direction and renews the mind to reject the lies of Satan.

3. SPIRIT ENCOUNTER

"And do not be drunk with wine, in which is dissipation; but be filled with the Spirit" (Ephesians 5:18, NKJV). A Spirit-filled life will maintain the victory and deliverance brought by a truth and power encounter. Paul taught the importance of the following:

1. Corporate worship (speaking to one another in psalms, hymns and spiritual songs, v. 19).
2. Private worship (making melody in your heart to the Lord, v. 19).
3. Thanksgiving (giving thanks to God, v. 20).
4. Submission (submitting to one another in the fear of God, v. 21).

Something wonderful and powerful happens when we live a life of worship, thanksgiving, and submission. Our worship to God is a constant confession before Him that in Christ we are complete. When we offer thanks to God in and for all things, that is a constant confession to Him that there exists no lack. Once we believe and embrace the truth of completeness, our hearts are settled, anxiety leaves, fires are rekindled, passion is ignited, and relationships are restored.

Thanksgiving for our spouse, our job, our position in life is a faith confession of praise to God that those things in our life are enough. We are complete through our union with Christ. Lack will always attempt to invade the ungrateful heart, bringing along with it doubts, suspicion, and fears. A sense of incompleteness or inadequacy will cause a lack of appreciation and thanksgiving.

Any lack that existed in the Church (the bride of Christ) was more than made up for by Christ as "he gave up his life for her to make her holy and clean, washed by baptism and God's word. He did this to present her to himself as a glorious church without a spot or wrinkle or any other blemish [no lack]. Instead, she will be holy and without fault. In the same way, husbands ought to love their wives as they love their own bodies" (Ephesians 5:25b-28a, NLT). Amazing, isn't it? A church without lack (fault or blemish) made holy by Christ who now rejoices over her and gives thanks to God for her. "Rejoice in the wife of your youth" (Proverbs 5:18b). By your loving her, sacrificing for her, she stands before you without lack. Giving thanks to God for her is your confession of contentment and praise to God, that she is more than enough. The goal is a Spirit-led relationship that says, "I live in spiritual, relational, and positional contentment because I am complete in Christ." In a Spirit-led relationship we do not have to live in anxiety. We can live in contentment created by thanksgiving. As Christ loved, washed, cleansed, and rejoiced over His Church, anything lacking was made complete. As men love, restore, heal, and rejoice over their wives, any lack or legitimate need is made complete, bringing great satisfaction and contentment in their lives. If husbands do for their wives as Christ did for the Church, their wives will be far more than they ever imagined. And a relationship without lack becomes completely secure.

Through union with Christ you can banish lack and be complete.

David Crispin has served as senior pastor of First Assembly Worship Center in Alamogordo, New Mexico, since 1988. Crispin was educated at Southwestern Assemblies of God University and ordained in 1983 in the West Texas District Council. He and his wife, Kathy, entered full-time pastoral ministry in 1977 and have served congregations in Rankin, Texas; Hobbs, New Mexico; and Midland, Texas (associate pastor).

Their current congregation has thrived in Alamogordo, despite the turnover in this military city, the home of Holloman Air Force Base. First Assembly has grown from 200 Sunday attendees in 1988 to 900 at present.

The Crispins come from Odessa, Texas, and have three children: Justin, Jennifer, and Tiffany.

17

LONELINESS
Giving Yourself Away

RUSSELL W. EGGERT

In the movie *Castaway*, Tom Hanks finds himself on a deserted island miles from anywhere with little to no hope of rescue. The experience is frightening as he realizes he has no way to contact loved ones or friends, and that this isolation may go on indefinitely. He is lonely to the point of painting a face on a ball, attaching grass for hair, giving it a name, and then talking to "Wilson" as if he were real. Yes, he even pretends that Wilson talks to him. Loneliness, in this case, drives a man to extreme actions to have some imaginary human contact.

Loneliness has always been an issue for man. In Genesis 2:18, "The Lord God said, 'It is not good for the man to be alone'" (NIV). Animals were not enough company, so God made him a suitable helper. Loneliness is a problem that almost everyone has struggled with at some time in his or her life. It can lead to depression, all types of inappropriate social behavior, and even to suicide.

What is loneliness?

Loneliness is a feeling. It is brought on by a sense of separation. Separation is not all about distance. Remember a time you were separated from someone you loved or your first experience as a homesick child. It didn't matter if you were 100 miles or just one block away, you may have shed tears because you missed your parents. I still vividly remember what it was like for me during the Vietnam conflict. I was thousands of miles away from the wife I loved and my infant son with the real possibility that I might never see them again. That sense of loneliness is deep and even painful. Many have been separated by war, armed service, business, an accident, even death. Whatever the reason, that feeling of being separated from the one you love is loneliness.

David, in Psalm 25:16, asked God to turn and be gracious, because he was lonely and afflicted. This was possibly penned on one of the occasions when he had to leave his family and his best friend, Jonathan, and hide in the wilderness from King Saul. In Psalm 68:6, we read that God sees the lonely and makes provision for them by setting them in families. David learned where to turn when he felt abandoned. God had surrounded him with people of like mind and faith.

Separation often brings a feeling of isolation. Is isolation always bad? There are times when isolation can become solitude. These opportunities are precious. All distractions are removed and now we are alone with God. This might be frightening for some, but what a wonderful opportunity to speak to Him, and more importantly to listen to that still small voice as He speaks to us. Alone does not always mean lonely. There is a song that we often sang in our churches that says, "He walks with me and He talks with me." It speaks of an intimacy that allows us to be physically alone, yet emotionally not lonely. There have been various times of separation from my wife and child, but intimacy with my wife has grown to where, even though we are separated by distance, we are not separated emotionally. I can be somewhere without her yet know how she would react to what I am experiencing. I am thinking of her, know where she will be, and know that she is also thinking of me. How much more important to have an intimate relationship with God so that we are never alone. He is the unseen One that walks by our side at all times, ever ready to assist, converse, direct or just be our companion. He is a Friend who sticks closer than a brother.

Strange that we can be lonely in a crowd. Loneliness is not determined by the number of people around us, but our emotional reaction to our personal circumstances. We can be lonely and unhappy in a crowd if people don't focus their attention on us. We wait for them to come and say hello or to start the conversation. Out of self-centeredness, we expect them to seek us out and make us feel important. Affliction can also play a part in loneliness. And physical discomfort can magnify our emotional weakness. The fact David was being chased by a king trying to kill him certainly increased his feelings of loneliness. I know that my loneliness was increased by my self-centeredness and my affliction. I wanted to get home to be with my family where I would be safe from anti-aircraft weapons and surface-to-air missiles. How about you? What is the source of your loneliness? Are you now or have you been separated from someone you love? Is your aloneness a product of your lifestyle? Have you left God out? Is your separation from others a product of alienation? Have you put up walls that others cannot penetrate? Hopefully, we have not alienated others with an attitude of superiority, self-righteousness, smugness, aloofness, or self-centeredness. That type of loneliness is self-inflicted.

What is the answer for loneliness? It seems quite simple. Companionship. Of course it is never that easy. The Bible and life both show very clearly that the wrong companions can lead to even greater problems. Where do I go, then, to find a solution for my loneliness? How about if we look at the example that Christ has set for us? At times He was lonely. In John 16:31,32, Jesus tells the disciples, "You will leave me all alone. Yet I am not alone, for my Father is with me." In Matthew 26:37-44 we find Jesus in the Garden praying alone. He returns to His disciples two times hoping they will be praying with and for Him. Alone, He prays the cup of sorrow He must soon drink might possibly be removed. This passage tells us His soul was overwhelmed with sorrow. Alone is Jesus Christ, although circled by men who have previously promised to give their lives so no harm would come to Him. But, moments later, He stands alone, betrayed and forsaken. Alone before His accusers, He is interrogated, slandered, beaten, humiliated, and crucified. "He could have called ten thousand angels, but He died alone for you and me," the song lyrics say. On the day He was crucified, two others hung there with Him. One thief would die cursing, but one would plead for mercy. Even hanging on the cross there was work to be done. Mercy is extended to the penitent thief, prophecy is fulfilled, and a mother's future is secured. The Scriptures indicate that Jesus, for a moment, even felt forsaken by the

Father. Loneliness . . . how did He overcome? The answer is by giving himself away. He gave His life. Even on the cross He was still giving. The Father gave His Son, and the Son makes it clear He has come to give His life as a ransom for many.

The key to overcoming loneliness is to follow the example of Jesus and give ourselves away. If we do that we will have little time to be self-centered. We will also see our afflictions differently, knowing we have the promise that He will always be with us and never forsake us (Hebrews 13:5). We are never alone, because He is with us. Romans chapter eight tells us that nothing can separate us from the love of Christ! Because the more you give yourself away, the more people respond to you. May we become like Jesus—a servant of others.

Loneliness. Most people experience it, even great heroes of the Bible and Christ himself. You can overcome it. Your separation from God is ended as soon as you ask for His mercy. He will be with you. Try following His example. Give yourself away!

Russel W. Eggert, D.Min., is senior pastor of Marlton Assembly of God in Marlton, New Jersey. He holds master's degrees in biblical literature from Assemblies of God Theological Seminary, Springfield, Missouri, and in educational administration from Rowan University, Glassboro, New Jersey. He received a doctor of ministries degree from Trinity Evangelical Divinity School, Deerfield, Illinois. He has been in ministry for 30 years. Eggert taught at Cape College of Theology and worked with people of Islamic and Hindu backgrounds in Cape Town, South Africa. He is presently on the Board of Trustees for Valley Forge Christian College, Phoenixville, Pennsylvania, and part of the Assemblies of God Commission on Christian Higher Education.

A former first lieutenant in the United States Air Force, Eggert was a fighter pilot who flew search and rescue missions. He is married to Carol and has three children and five grandchildren.

18

TEMPTATION

A Deadly Game to Play

MICHAEL GOLDSMITH

"Tag! You're it!" The joyful sounds of laughter and shriek-ing voices of delight overflow a backyard filled with children engaged in the timeless game of tag. Children in every generation and every corner of the world have spent long afternoons passing a summer's day with a good old-fashioned round of tag. Kids involved in this wonderful game usually have a great time until someone is accused of cheating—mostly, by running out of bounds.

Temptation is Satan's game of tag—his way of trying to cause us to sin against God. However, unlike the child's game of tag, Satan wins by causing us to run *out of bounds*. His goal is to lure us across the boundary lines God has established.

The rules of tag are simple, with minor variations from place to place. One person is designated *it*. The boundaries are decided. "Home" is the designated safe place where every player but *it* is trying to arrive without being tagged by *it*. During a round of tag, the objective is for everyone to try to make it home without being tagged. If you touch home base without being tagged, you're safe for that round. If, however, you're tagged by the designated *it*, you become *it* for the next round. Whoever is *it* remains *it* until a new *it* is tagged by the current *it*.

Usually, *it* closes his or her eyes and gives the players a chance to take their place in the yard. When the game begins, *it* is standing between the players and home. Everyone begins running all over the yard trying to make it home without being tagged. *It* is desperately trying to tag anyone to be released from being *it* in the next round. Everything goes well as long as everyone stays inside the boundaries. When someone runs outside a boundary, they are cheating. When the heat is on and *it* is breathing down your neck, everyone is very tempted to do whatever it takes to stay in the game, including running out of bounds.

God has clearly designated boundary lines for successful living. These boundaries are given to us throughout the Word of God. Satan uses temptation to attempt to move us beyond the safe boundaries. When we stay within the clearly marked boundaries given to us by God, we are safe and play the game of life according to the rules. Once we cross a boundary, it is no longer temptation; it becomes sin.

Genesis 39 gives a vivid visual illustration of temptation. It's the story of Joseph's temptation with Potiphar's wife. While this was specifically a sexual temptation, the account provides us with principles applicable to every temptation. *Do not skim this chapter just because you are not specifically tempted sexually.* Everyone faces temptation. Look for the general principles that apply to every temptation.

Scripture is filled with accounts of men and women who ran out of bounds into sin. Joseph, however, was both powerfully tempted and successfully resistant. Though he paid a heavy price, he successfully overcame temptation, did not compromise his integrity, kept his walk with God pure, and resisted the desire to go out of bounds.

There are five principles of temptation we can ascertain from the example of Joseph.

First, there is temptation's *personal appeal.* Genesis 39:6 states, "Joseph was handsome in form and appearance" (NASV). Joseph was a well-built, handsome man. In addition, Potiphar was captain of Pharaoh's bodyguards. Someone of this stature would likely have had a beautiful wife. What a deadly combination—a beautiful woman of power tempting a well-built, handsome slave.

Joseph's temptation began in the area of personal appeal. God has placed acceptable desires (hungers) within each of our lives. What is appealing to one person may or may not be appealing to another. The devil understands all human desire and has an arsenal of tactics to use as tools of temptation. The work begins with personal and normal hungers. Temptation becomes sin when we cross the boundary line of God-given desires. The famous seven deadly sins—pride, envy, anger, sloth, greed, gluttony, and lust—are all illustrations of physical desires gone *out of bounds.*

It has often been said that one's greatest strength can also be one's greatest weakness. Satan combined several good desires in the life of Joseph into an explosive prescription for sin. Joseph was far removed from his home and was alone, thus any relationship would be very appealing. Joseph had an unmet need for relationship, which could be accommodated with this woman's advances. This was not just another slave, but Potiphar's wife—someone of significant position. Using Potiphar's wife to tempt Joseph, Satan was essentially attempting to dignify sin. Satan loves to mask temptation behind the veil of respectability, dignity, position, and status. Potiphar's wife—what an appeal to the male ego. Temptation always appeals to our egos. It is also secretive. Potiphar's wife made her advances when no one else was around. Potiphar left the house to oversee his business. The other slaves were engaged in their household responsibilities. Joseph and Potiphar's wife were now completely alone in the house.

The personal appeal of sin is usually masked by these characteristics: appealing to an unmet need; appearing to be dignified; appealing to our egos; and the promise of privacy, combining with desires deep within us. The more these align, the more deadly the temptation concoction will become.

Second, there is temptation's *persuasive appetite*. Genesis 39:7 notes that Potiphar's wife "looked with desire at Joseph." Here was an attractive woman alone every day with an attractive man. Perhaps it started with a glance. Casual glances advanced to longing, tempting gazes as she allowed her appetite to become stronger.

The temptations we entertain, either visually or mentally, are the ones that give us the most trouble. The more we entertain temptation, the greater the chance of succumbing to sin. Scripture gives compelling evidence of temptations turning to sin because of what was "seen." Eve "*saw* that the tree was good for food, and that it was a delight to the eyes" (Genesis 3:6). Lot "lifted up his eyes and *saw* all the valley of the Jordan, that it was well watered everywhere" (Genesis 13:10). Judah "*saw* there a daughter of a certain Canaanite whose name was Shua; and he took her and went in to her" (Genesis 38:2). David "*saw* a woman bathing; and the woman was very beautiful in appearance" (2 Samuel 11:2). All these people fell into the grip of sin by entertaining the persuasive appetite of visual temptation. It is not only what we see visually; what we "see" mentally has an equally compelling appetite. One of the tricks of temptation is to cause us to mentally "see" a satisfying end by indulging in temptation. Sin is the result of crossing the boundary line from "seeing" to appeasing the appetite.

Third is temptation's *persistent attraction.* Joseph felt the force of temptation growing through the persistent efforts of Potiphar's wife. Genesis 39:10 reminds us "she spoke to Joseph day after day." Temptation does not relent easily. Steady, certain, unending drops of water can eventually wear away the greatest boulder. It is not the first temptation that trips us. It's the 50th or 100th time the same temptation visits us we finally cave in to sinful behavior. Imagine the day-after-day wear on Joseph as Potiphar's wife, dressed seductively, finds Joseph and speaks to him every day. It would be difficult to believe her repeated appeals were not wearing down Joseph's resistance.

We must never conclude we have forever defeated temptation simply because we have successfully resisted *once.* Even Jesus Christ endured repeated temptations. Luke 4:13 tells us, "When the devil had finished every temptation, he departed from Him until an opportune time." Note that Christ faced "every temptation" of the devil. Yes, the devil departed, but only to watch and wait for an "opportune time," a better moment.

Mark these words. Temptation will return! It does not give up easily or quickly. It is patient, deliberate, and methodical. We may have resisted today, but tomorrow is another day. Never assume today's victory is ultimate. We should use each day to strengthen our spiritual life for the next round of future temptations.

Fourth, there is temptation's *penetrating aggression*. When Potiphar's wife realized her repeated attempts to bring Joseph out of bounds were not working, she decided to turn up the heat. She became more aggressive. Genesis 39:12 declares, "She caught him by his garment, saying, 'Lie with me!'" By grabbing his clothing, she closed the gap between the two of them. Temptation is constantly working to close the gap between us and sin.

Temptation is never content to make passive attempts. Forcing us out of bounds is the constant goal. Therefore, temptation invades and assaults our comfort zone, attempting to pressure us to cross over the line. Just as certainly as Joseph felt the physical pressure of Potiphar's wife's demands, so the devil brings every possible force and pressure to bear on us. For example, an employer may pressure an employee to falsify company reports or peers may pressure us by advocating social drinking as acceptable behavior.

Finally, there are temptation's *prevailing alternatives*. When it comes to temptation, we have two choices: give in and sin, or resist. Joseph resisted and won this battle with temptation. "How then could I do this great evil, and sin against God?" (Genesis 39:9). Joseph kept God in the picture in his fight against temptation. The condition of our relationship with God has more to do with our ability to resist temptation than any other factor. There is an undeniable correlation in which loving God has moral implications for personal behavior. Adam and Eve sinned against God; their son Cain, in turn, killed his brother Abel. Once the relationship with God was damaged and broken, the residual effects caused the relationships of man to deteriorate. Man sinned against God, then man sinned against himself and mankind.

Consider the Ten Commandments. The first four affect our relationship with God; the final six affect our relationships with others. The Great Commandment (John 13:34), implies loving God results in loving humanity. First John teaches we cannot love God, whom we have not seen, and hate humanity with whom we interact on a daily basis (1 John 4:20). Ephesians 1:15 teaches that our faith in God results in healthy human relationships. In another setting, Jesus taught the disciples that responding in healthy community relationships with one another is proof of one's love for God. Our relationship with God bears on our personal and moral conduct in life.

Joseph and David both faced the same temptation. Joseph left. David looked. The defining point of difference had to do with the condition of their relationship with God at the moment of temptation.

Temptation appealed to Joseph in three important ways. First, it *appealed to a longing for power.* Joseph, from his youth, had dreams of personal greatness. Even in Potiphar's house he ascended to the highest position under Potiphar. If Joseph could have Potiphar's wife, he would, in essence, fulfill a desire for power. Second, it had an *affirming appeal,* being wanted by Potiphar's wife! Think of how seductive that must have been for Joseph. Here was a young man whom a beautiful woman found desirable. Third, it *promised to fulfill the human need for intimacy.* Temptation baited Joseph with the promise to meet his unmet need for human intimacy through sexual involvement. Similarly, temptation promises to meet the unmet needs in our lives.

Navigating temptation is serious business. It's not just a child's game of tag. It's a very real threat designed to push us *out of bounds* into sin. We can resist temptation by acknowledging our own desires, building our relationship with God, and staying alert to the boundaries God has established for us.

Don't be caught out of bounds. It will disqualify you in this life and in the one to come.

Michael Goldsmith is senior pastor of Broken Arrow Assembly of God in Broken Arrow, Oklahoma, where he has served for the last four years. The church ministries include a large preschool and a K-10 elementary school. Goldsmith is leading the church in a multi-million dollar relocation to 40 acres of debt-free property. Goldsmith has 19 years of ministry experience which include nine years as a youth pastor. He served as assistant youth director for the Arkansas District and spoke at youth camps and conferences. He also pastored First Assembly of God in Siloam Springs, Arkansas, for six years, during which the church more than doubled in attendance. He is the author of numerous newspaper and magazine articles and has a published chapter in Living Like Jesus. *Goldsmith is a graduate of Southwestern Assemblies of God University in Waxahachie, Texas, and is a master's of practical theology candidate at Oral Roberts University, Tulsa, Oklahoma. He and his wife, Debbie, have two daughters: Abby and Sarah.*

19

ADVERSITY

What to Do When the Storms Come

JIM FRANKLIN

As a boy growing up in northeastern Oklahoma, I remember sunny afternoons when the warm day air would begin to mix with the cool night air and a thunderstorm would arise. These storms would come up suddenly out of nowhere with darkening clouds, lightning, and thunder. Sometimes they'd produce a dreaded tornado.

That's the way life can be. Things can be going great, looking good, and suddenly a dark cloud arises, and before you know it you're in the middle of what seems to be a life-threatening storm. What do we do when those storms come? How do we survive?

Mark 4:35-41 says Jesus and His disciples were out in a boat and a great, life-threatening storm arose. They knew they could not survive on their own ability.

Maybe you're facing such a situation in your life. This story offers several key principles that can help you make it through your storms.

First, we must learn that *things change*. When these men started out in the boat with Jesus, it was a beautiful day. Everything was smooth sailing. But suddenly the storm came. Everyone will face trouble in life. If you are in smooth times, get ready. Things change. But, if you are in a storm, hang on, because things change. That's the essence of life. Nothing stays the same. The goal in life is not to avoid storms, but to make it through them.

Second, note that *when the storm came these men were following Jesus*. Some assume if they are following Jesus everything is going to be smooth. But, just because you are following Jesus doesn't mean that you will not face trouble.

When problems and difficulties come, many people make comments like this: "Well, I must be doing something wrong or God would be blessing me right now." Or they'll rationalize the problem by saying, "I must be doing something right because the devil sure is fighting me." You can't have it both ways. You don't determine the will of God by circumstances—whether good or bad—but only by the Word of God. Jesus directed His disciples to get into the boat and go to the other side. Allowing your feelings or circumstances to dictate God's will, will make you more confused than a termite in a yo-yo. God's word to them was that they would pass to the other side. If you're facing a storm and you are following what God has told you to do, don't give up. Stay on board. Don't look at the waves. Keep your eyes upon Jesus.

My wife and I were ministering in Hawaii and we took a day off for some recreation. In Honolulu we took a sailboat dinner tour out into the harbor. We boarded that boat with several others who were vacationing, including a lot of honeymooners. As we sailed into the harbor, a storm arose. The boat started to rock. I looked around the ship and saw people not very concerned about looking perfect for their mate. All they were concerned about now was keeping their lunch down. They were turning several shades of green, and heading to the back of the boat. (I don't think they were looking at the fish as they hung their heads over the side.) I turned to my wife, Cyndi. Suddenly we recognized the same feeling was coming upon us. We were beginning to get seasick. The waves were beating against the boat as it rocked back and forth and we were doing everything we could to try to talk each other out of getting sick.

The captain of the boat gave us some advice. He said, "Instead of looking at the waves or the boat or people around you, what you need to do is look at the horizon. Find an object on land, and set your sights on it." The highest point there was Diamond Head. So we stood at the front of the boat and fixed our eyes upon it. We looked like a couple of bird dogs at the front of that boat. Determined not to take our eyes off of that rock, by the grace of God, we were able to make it to dry land. Later, I thought, *That's exactly what we need to do when the storms come. We need to set our eyes upon the Solid Rock, Jesus Christ, and He'll make sure we get to the other side.* The key is what we do in the "in-between" time, from the storm's start to its finish.

These disciples were in a terrible situation. The Bible says the boat was taking on water. I'm not much of a sailor, but I do know that when your boat is filling up with water, it's not a good thing. The disciples were being overwhelmed by the circumstance of the sea. Do you ever feel overwhelmed, like you're taking on too much and you can't handle it? If so, recognize that you *can't* handle it. It will take something bigger than you to get you through that situation. Often our problem is that we try to handle it, and we end up losing it. We need God in our lives. When you're in the middle of a storm you see things differently. Your perspective changes. Those people on the boat in Hawaii suddenly weren't concerned about their appearance; they just wanted the storm to end.

Here's what the disciples did to make it through the storm:

First, when they *knew* they needed help, the disciples remembered Jesus was on the boat. At first they had tried everything but relying on Jesus. Perhaps you've relied on what you can do and it didn't work. With all of your talent, you may have forgotten Who's on board. With all of your programs, possessions, people, and position, you relied on yourself and forgot your Life-Preserver—Jesus Christ. He is the only One who can save us, deliver us, heal us, baptize us, free us, put our marriages back together, bring our kids home, stop the violence in the streets. We'd better remember He's the only One on board who can save us. You're not alone, God is on your side, and though you walk through the valley of the shadow of death, you don't have to fear—He is with you.

Second, the disciples went to where Jesus was. The Bible describes that He was in the hinder part of the boat, so they had to go to where He was to awaken Him. God doesn't leave you in your time of storm . . . but maybe you've left God. Perhaps you're so busy you've forgotten Him. Where did you leave Jesus? Perhaps it's your prayer closet, because you stopped praying. When you discover where you left Him, go back to the place where you knew your relationship with God was secure, where fear left you and faith was still present.

The disciples found Jesus asleep in the midst of the storm. That demonstrates great faith and security. It's not when everything is going right that our faith is tested. When someone can rest in the midst of a storm, an illness, or a sudden tragedy, that's a person of great faith. It's easy to believe God when things are going well, but it takes great faith to believe God when things are going badly, in the midst of a storm.

Third, the disciples called upon Jesus. They called Him "Master." It's not enough knowing Jesus is there; you need to call on Him. I know where the pizza parlor is, but until I call them I'm not going to get my pizza delivered. It's the same way with the power of prayer. We recognize that Jesus is in our lives, but to appropriate His help we must call upon Him. Jesus doesn't want to be your co-pilot; He wants to be your Pilot. The disciples knew they didn't just need counsel, or an opinion, they needed a Master. If you're going to make it through the storms of life, you need to make Him the Master of your life.

What was the result? Jesus got up, stepped to the front of the boat, spoke to the winds and the waves, and there was a great calm. Note the use of that word "great." In describing the storm earlier it was referred to as a "great" storm. This word describes a storm that was not only raging on top of the water but was also raging beneath the water. It even suggests the earth was shaking. Many times the storms we face trouble us on and beneath the surface. Jesus stood amid the flashes of lightning and rolling waves, with darkness all around. He spoke a word, and immediately it was calm. The boat is no longer tossing back and forth. The sun perhaps begins to shine again. The wind ceases.

It can happen just that way for you. No matter how great the storm or turmoil is, if you put Jesus in control of your life He can speak a word, and immediately the situation can be turned around. I've experienced that so many times in my life. After I've received peace and assurance from the Lord, suddenly what was darkness and turmoil transformed into faith and produced a calming in my spirit. Maybe the circumstances around me did not change but something inside me did. That's what Jesus can do in your storm. He has a great calm for you.

"What manner of man is this?" He's the One that demons obey. He opens blinded eyes, forgives prostitutes, calls the dead back to life, takes the vilest of sinners and makes them saints. He can take you where you are and lift you to the highest heavens. He will fill your life with meaning and direction. He'll baptize you with the Holy Spirit. That's what manner of man He is!

If you're facing the storms of life, remember Jesus is on board. Go to Him. Return to your first love. Call upon Him, and make Him the master of your life, and then, as these disciples recognized, the word of the Lord will come to pass, and you'll make it to the other side.

James H. Franklin is a native-born Oklahoman who has served in churches in Oklahoma, New Mexico and California. In 1993 Franklin began serving as senior pastor at Cornerstone Church in Fresno, California. Within two years the

Sunday morning services tripled in attendance. Attendance has spiraled from 300 to over 3,000 in less than 9 years as the church has become the most racially diverse in the city. Pastor Franklin has one of the longest running and highest rated local television programs in the Valley, called Cornerstone Live.

Cornerstone is recognized for its passionate efforts to win the lost. Their feeding ministry distributed food to more than 650,000 people in the California Valley in one year alone. Pastor Franklin's heart to reach out to the hurting has culminated in ministries to the homeless, prostitutes, gang members and those behind prison walls.

Under Pastor Franklin's leadership Cornerstone is playing a key part in the revitalization of downtown Fresno, with ownership of more than two city blocks. The 1,600-seat Historic Wilson Theatre, built in 1927, serves as the sanctuary.

Franklin and his wife, Cyndi, have three children: Jessica, Nathan and James.

20

GUILT AND REGRET
Defeating the Past

CARL D. KEYES

The phone call came at 1 P.M. "George didn't come home last night," the voice said.

"When was the last time someone saw him?" I asked. After 15 minutes of trying to figure things out, I thought for the first time that George's habit had gotten the best of him. Eleven days of anguish later, my worst fear came true. My brother of 44 years wasn't ever coming home. His wife and friends had called me numerous times over the past three years and begged me to help. Occasionally I would respond with a trip to their home, only to find a remorseful and tortured soul. I felt there was nothing I could do. But after George had left this earth I realized there were a thousand things I could have done.

Guilt and regret. They don't ever seem to go away. Sure, there are seasons of forgetting, times of victory, and even days of denial, but when the truth is told, I still feel like it was my fault. "I should have done more" or "If only." These are the types of phrases that plummet a person into the vortex of guilt and clothe them in a garment of regret. It is a place of alienation, loneliness, and depression. "I will lift up my eyes to the hills—from whence comes my help?" (Psalm 121:1, NKJV). You look, but can't see any help. As I searched the Scriptures for relief, I found an interesting passage in 2 Corinthians 12. I believe God was showing me how He takes "all things [and] work[s them] together for good to those who love God, to those who are the called according to His purpose" (Romans 8:28).

Paul had a "thorn in the flesh," a harassing pain, an emotional or spiritual difficulty, some relentless and bother-some ache. The Scripture tells us it was a "messenger of Satan" (2 Corinthians 12:7). When we translate "messenger," it comes up "angel." The words "of Satan" tell us it was an angel of darkness, or a demon. External supernatural forces were at work harassing Paul. They had become a thorn in his flesh and were "buffeting" him. Buffeting refers to the waves slapping against a bulkhead. This relentless assault by a demonic influence drove Paul to speak to the Lord about it three times.

I wonder if Satan was playing on Paul's past. In Acts 8 we see that "Saul was in hearty agreement with putting him [Stephen] to death" (v. 1, NASB). Stephen, a man "of wisdom" (Acts 6:3), "faith" (v. 5), "grace and power" (v. 8), the Scripture says, was brutally stoned. And Saul, who was later called Paul, stood by and watched. Could this have been the external supernatural force doing an evil work in the life of Paul? This demon who would not let him forget what he had done? A constant reminder of who he used to be? God was using Paul in a magnificent way. He was giving him special revelations, using him to teach, to testify, and to establish the Early Church, to mention a few things. But this thorn in the flesh which buffeted him kept rising up in Paul's life and ministry. We all anguish over past sins. We all wish we could go back and change a hundred different things in our life, but there are some memories of the past that will not go away.

It was December 30, 1981. My two-year marriage to Donna was racing to an end. My poor state of mind, constant drinking and drug use, drug trafficking, and the mental abuse I afflicted on my wife were leading us to a divorce. A friend invited us away for a weekend and, as the Lord would have it, two days later we were standing at an altar in Augusta, Maine, giving our hearts to the Lord. New Year's Day 1982 I was totally delivered of drugs and alcohol and never had the smallest desire to do them again. We then began setting our sights on a new life. I heard Dr. Mark Rutland say that "there is no greater patriot than a refugee." How right he is! Donna and I now have two boys, Matthew and Ryan, have been married 23 years, and pastor a wonderful church in mid-town Manhattan. That's a great story! On the other hand, my brother George—the best man at my wedding, the first to come and help when someone was in need, the first to take his last dollar and give it away—struggled with a drug addiction that eventually killed him. You see, he also received Christ, but was not totally delivered as I was. He was terrorized by a cocaine addiction every waking moment of his much-too-short life. I was set free of a lifestyle that eventually would have gotten the better of me. And George, well, he battled it out at the altar of his church every Sunday. I'm alive with a beautiful wife and two fine young men for sons. He left behind a wonderful wife and two boys, ages 2 and 4. Talk about guilt.

So, why was I delivered and George wasn't? I do not know. But there is one thing that I do know. Life isn't fair! God never promised us fairness; He promised grace. Guilt and regret will not go away until you hear and receive the word of the Lord. "My grace is sufficient for you, for power is perfected in weakness" (2 Corinthians 12:9). Yes, there will be difficulties. Yes, you will have regrets. Yes, you will have guilt heaped upon you as if Satan himself placed it there. But God has given us the power to overcome these feelings through His wonderful grace. Grace poured out on us through the blood of His own Son. Grace so great and love so wonderful that no "thorn in the flesh," no "messenger of Satan," no relentless "buffeting" of the enemy can rob us of these gifts! And when we ensconce ourselves in these tools of the enemy we give our victory away and deny the power of His grace.

King David suffered with similar symptoms of guilt and regret. He came to the realization of his sin at the hand of the prophet Nathan, when he pointed his finger at David in 2 Samuel 12:7 and said, "You are the man!" Conviction fell upon David and he repented of his sins. But the guilt was eating him up on the inside. He allowed himself to be cursed and scorned by Shimei in 2 Samuel 16 and walked away from his God-given calling as he dealt with his failures as a king, as God's servant, as a husband, and as a father. David cast himself out of the society God had placed him in. He felt worthless, empty, and contemptible. He had dishonored his position and his people. He had reached the bottom. Now the only place to look was up. David worked his way through his anguish and, somehow, through the clouds of his own despair, he encouraged himself and once again saw a glimmer of his merciful and forgiving God. Needless to say, God never gave up on David. He saw a redemptive quality in him when David could see nothing but his own failures.

Eventually, in Psalm 32:5, David mentions three important actions: (1) He acknowledges his sin, (2) he does not hide his iniquity, and (3) he confesses his transgressions. Afterward David comes to the understanding that God not only forgave him, but He also released him of "the guilt of [his] sin" (v. 5). The power of God's grace is greater than the guilt of our sin. Now this is worth rejoicing about! In verse 7 David says, "You shall surround me with songs of deliverance" (NKJV). Then in verse 10 we read, "But he who trusts in the LORD, lovingkindness shall surround him" (NASV). David finally sees his value in the Kingdom, even with his shortcomings. Looking at ourselves in a guilt-ridden manner is not the way the Lord looks at us. He thinks so much of us and loves us so much that it was worth the life of His Son. His love is without end and without boundaries. We are the ones who limit His grace and love by not receiving all that He has for us. We must reach down deep inside ourselves and begin to see ourselves as God sees us.

There is an old fable about a girl who was held prisoner in a tower by a witch. The witch kept her there by telling her she was so ugly that no one would be able to stand looking at her. As the years went by, Rapunzel's hair grew and grew so that the witch would get to the top of the tower by saying, "Rapunzel, Rapunzel, let down your hair that I may climb the golden stair." Her hair would come down and the witch would climb up. A handsome prince came by one day and overheard the witch's command. He waited for her to leave and gave Rapunzel the same command. The hair came down and he climbed up. What he saw was the most beautiful woman he had ever seen, but Rapunzel would not believe him. Then he said, "Look deep into my eyes so that you may see yourself." And when she did, she saw the reflection of her own beauty in the eyes of her savior. And the prince carried her off to be his wife and, of course, they lived happily ever after.

This is what God is telling us today. Look deep into the eyes of the Savior and you shall see the reflection of your own beauty. The apostle Paul did it. King David did it. I did it. You can do it too. Just trust Him.

Carl D. Keyes is the senior pastor of Glad Tidings Tabernacle in New York, New York, a church with a citywide network of cell groups. Keyes and his wife, Donna, have over 50 years of combined leadership and ministry experience and are excellent communicators to this generation. Their missionary spirit has led them to begin works that extend from the inner city of Brooklyn and the Bronx to South Africa, Zimbabwe, and Ghana.

The Keyeses reside in Manhattan in New York City with their two children, Matthew and Ryan.

21

CHILD ABUSE

Replacing Heartache With Joy

WAYNE TESCH

Every person experiences pain, suffering and grief—troubles that we do not deserve or did not expect. You may feel that the ache of losing someone you love, the heartbreak of relationships, and the stress of financial problems place too high a price on life. During difficulty we wonder if we will ever recover, but in these seasons of doubt we must look to God for the strength, courage, and healing we so desperately need. He is waiting with loving and compassionate arms outstretched. "He healeth the broken in heart, and bindeth up their wounds" (Psalm 147:3, KJV).

No one is exempt from pain—but those times of pain can bring beautiful communion with God. We can learn the depth of strength and peace found *only* in Him. "Peace I leave with you, my peace I give unto you: not as the world giveth, give I unto you. Let not your heart be troubled, neither let it be afraid" (John 14:27).

No matter what your trial, no matter how unbearable your grief, no matter how deep your pain, God loves you and knows exactly how you feel. He wants to replace your heartache with joy. "To console those who mourn in Zion, to give them beauty for ashes, the oil of joy for mourning, the garment of praise for the spirit of heaviness" (Isaiah 61:3, NKJV).

I have seen it happen! I have seen God miraculously at work in lives that have been ravaged by cruelty and despair. At Royal Family Kids' Camps across the country, we see the worst kind of pain and violation—child abuse.

Too many precious children bear the physical and emotional scars of hatred, physical and sexual abuse, and neglect. Every summer, we try to give some of the more than 3 million children in this country who suffer from child abuse a week they can call their own—a week of fun, of love and safety, of hope and trust. During these special church-sponsored camps, we see how deep the emotional scars can go. We see the high price of child abuse. But we also have the opportunity to see God's healing power.

God's strength and encouragement are never more apparent than in the eyes of a child. Every scar on their little hearts and souls can be soothed with the healing salve of Jesus Christ. And God can bring healing and comfort to your battle scars as well. If you are hurting, the following scars may look familiar. Take comfort in God's healing salves. His promises hold true no matter what your age or circumstance.

SCAR #1: DEATH OF TRUST

Several years ago while serving as a camp counselor, I met Danny. I tried every way that I could to show him I cared for him and that he could trust me. One day, I found Danny in the corner of the dining room, curled in a ball, his head between his legs. I sat down beside him and noticed he was crying. I melted.

Through tear-filled eyes, Danny looked up at me and asked, "Are you going to hit me now?"

I was somewhat taken back. Very gently I said, "No. Why would I ever want to hit you?"

He quietly responded, "'Cause everyone who has ever loved me has hit me." We both sat there and cried.

Because so often child abuse and neglect involve the child's caregiver, trust is one of the major casualties in the battle. The first person children trust in their lives is the hand that rocks the cradle. What then becomes of trust if that hand also breaks, bruises, and maims?

HEALING SALVE #1: GOD'S LOVE

If your trust has been violated, you can take comfort and solace in God's healing love. "For I am persuaded, that neither death, nor life, nor angels, nor principalities, nor powers, nor things present, nor things to come, Nor height, nor depth, nor any other creature, shall be able to separate us from the love of God, which is in Christ Jesus our Lord" (Romans 8:38,39, KJV).

Love is a powerful potion. And no love is greater than God's love. When we allow the love of God to flow through our lives, there is no limit to its healing power!

A little boy sauntered up to one of our camp "grandmas" and asked the question that many of the campers ask: "Grandma, how much are you getting paid?"

Astonished, Grandma responded, "What do you mean?"

The little boy sighed and said, "Grandma, everybody who takes care of me gets paid. My foster parents get paid. My social worker. My counselor. Everybody who loves me gets paid!"

Grandma knelt down and looked him in the eye and said, "Everybody at this camp is volunteering. We do it because we care about you. You are special to us!"

Remember, Jesus Christ paid the price for *you* and asks *no* price in return. You are loved beyond measure.

If you are going through a hard time or trying to overcome the pain of your childhood, please realize that God wants to wrap you in His arms of love and bring peace to your heart. Just as our hearts go out to these hurting children, God's heart is pricked when you feel pain. He is your loving Father; rely on Him and rest in His eternal love.

SCAR #2: PERPETUAL ANGER

Children in our society are taught to honor adults. Because of the size difference between children and adults, kids realize they can't defend themselves against an adult attacker. It is impossible for children to vindicate themselves on an adult who is abusing them. The result is a perpetual, pent-up anger that has no place for expression.

As adults, we know that pent-up anger must be released or it will work itself out in ways that are generally not related to the subject of the anger. Abused children handle their anger in the same way. Only God's loving presence can melt away the anger of these children. If you have been wronged, release your anger into God's hands. He will replace it with joy and peace.

HEALING SALVE #2: GOD'S PRESENCE

It is nothing less than miraculous to see the transformation in the lives of these children in the presence of God. Only God can give a peace that passes all understanding in the face of cruelty and pain. In God's presence, anger and rage can be erased—if you let them. Your Heavenly Father does not want you to remain a slave to anger and hate. He wants you to feel the joy of giving your troubles completely to Him.

For abandoned, abused, and neglected 7- to 11-year-olds, Royal Family Kids' Camp gives that release. Camp means games, crafts, swimming, love from caring counselors, great new memories, camp songs, but most of all a personal encounter with God! Anger and fear can be replaced with God's presence and security. "For he hath said, I will never leave thee, nor forsake thee. So that we may boldly say, The Lord is my helper, and I will not fear what man shall do unto me" (Hebrews 13:5,6).

Remember God's eternal presence in *your* life when you think your world is spinning out of control. Place your anger in His capable hands.

SCAR #3: SELF-HATRED

The developmental years of children's lives determine their self-image. Young children tend to regard any pain or unpleasantness in their lives as their own fault. Many abused children believe the abuse happens because they are in some way bad or have done something wrong—particularly because much abuse happens in the name of punishment for misdeeds. If abused children believe that abuse is their fault because they are bad, they often abandon themselves to this "badness" and let it become a self-fulfilling prophecy. Like these precious children, if you feel beyond hope or help, look to God. He brings hope to the hopeless through the compassionate hands of His people.

HEALING SALVE #3: GOD'S HOPE

"When my father and my mother forsake me, then the LORD will take care of me" (Psalm 27:10, NKJV). The church can become the arms of the Lord taking care of neglected children and be part of the healing process. We are His hands of compassion, His arms of security and love. We can give hope—and in giving hope to others, it returns to us. We reap what we sow!

One time I was traveling Interstate 29 north from Kansas City to St. Joseph, Missouri, when an unusual sight caught my attention. Three red-tailed hawks were sitting on fence posts, not in the trees or on the tops of telephone poles where hawks usually perch. When I described the scene to the pastor of First Christian Church in St. Joseph where I was heading, he said the hawks had become "buzzardized." Instead of flying at high altitudes, like the great aerial hunters they were designed to be, the hawks of that region are content with perching on fence posts close to the highway. The fence posts provide easy access to "roadkill"—animals that have been run over by cars. He calls it "buzzard mentality," waiting for someone else to do the work. Some Christians, although created and designed by God to reach great heights and accomplish great deeds, are satisfied to sit in a pew and wait for others to do the ministry. They have allowed themselves to become buzzardized. Not so with the people involved in Royal Family Kids' Camps. Rather than sitting on the fence posts waiting to hear about God's wonderful healing for abused children, they are actively involved in making a difference in children's lives. Children like Tiffany.

Tiffany came to camp as a frightened 10-year-old. The little girl had lived with her paranoid-schizophrenic mother in cars, in cheap hotel rooms, and with abusive men. She had been malnourished and physically, emotionally, and sexually abused—always hoping someone would rescue her. At camp she found hope and her future. "I had never known that there was a God who really loved me and wanted me as His own to love," she said. "I realized that I need Him, and I wanted the incredible love and life that He offers as a free gift." While at camp, Tiffany was inspired to use her voice to help people. She kept that dream. Now as a university student, she studies voice therapy and plans to work with trauma victims. She has also worked at Royal Family Kids' Camps helping other kids.

As a child, Tiffany—like thousands of other abused children—found comfort and hope through the manifestation of God's love at Royal Family Kids' Camps. Through the more than 20,000 children who have attended our camps, we see God's help and care in action.

We see Him walking through the troubled times with them.

We see Him giving them positive memories to replace the pain and scars.

No matter what *your* situation, what *your* scar, what price *you* have paid, *you* can also find healing and encouragement in the Word of God. "I waited patiently for the Lord; he turned to me and heard my cry. He lifted me out of the slimy pit, out of the mud and mire; he set my feet on a rock and gave me a firm place to stand. He put a new song in my mouth, a hymn of praise to our God" (Psalm 40:1-3, NIV).

Rest assured, Jesus Christ will give you the strength and encouragement you need during the most troubling times of your life!

Wayne Tesch is the founder of Royal Family Kids' Camps, Inc., a nonprofit ministry that has developed a nationwide network of camps for abused and neglected children.

Tesch earned a B.A. from Evangel University in Springfield, Missouri, a master's in theological studies and church leadership from Vanguard University in Costa Mesa, California, and pursued graduate studies in health science at the State University of New York in Brockport, New York.

He has served as senior associate pastor at Newport-Mesa Christian Center, Costa Mesa, California, and two terms as a presbyter for the Assemblies of God Southern California District. Tesch was an adjunct professor of religion and physical education at Vanguard University and a religion fellowship instructor and soccer coach at Evangel University.

He was an appointed Southern California District home missionary for abused, abandoned and neglected children of America.

His published books include Unlocking the Secret World—A Unique Christian Ministry to Abused, Abandoned & Neglected Children *and* Moments Matter—The Stories of Royal Family Kids' Camps. *He has received several awards, including Distinguished Alumnus, Evangel University, 2000.*

Tesch and his wife, Diane, have been married for 35 years and have one married daughter, Renee, and two granddaughters.

22

ANGER

Letting Go of Wrath

HUBERT A. MORRIS

Road rage. Air rage. Domestic violence. These are frightening examples of a massive problem that afflicts our modern culture—the inappropriate display of anger.

In his book *Faded Glory,* Dr. H. Maurice Lednicky states, "The anger that has developed from not following scriptural principles in the home has found expression in mass murders in the classroom, vandalism for no reason, and a sullen, rebellious attitude toward parental authority. Drug and alcohol use have found the vulnerable on the elementary school campus."[1]

People today are struggling with deep inner frustrations that give vent to worse problems when they bubble forth.

NOT FOOLISH BUT WISE

The Book of Proverbs speaks clearly to this issue. "A fool gives full vent to his anger, but a wise man keeps himself under control" (Proverbs 29:11, NIV). "Like a city whose walls are broken down is a man who lacks self-control" (Proverbs 25:28). "An angry man stirs up dissension, and a hot-tempered one commits many sins" (Proverbs 29:22).

Anger can be turned into a good thing if we harness it properly. However, it appears that anger will always develop into a deeper emotional and physical problem for the person who ends his or her day and goes to sleep while still angry. "'In your anger do not sin.' Do not let the sun go down while you are still angry, and do not give the devil a foothold" (Ephesians 4:26,27). We need to deal with anger more easily and more quickly. We must make a choice to let go of anger that has within it unforgiveness, resentment, or revenge.

DISASTER FOR MOSES

Disaster can happen because of impulsive, angry reactions. Moses learned this lesson when leading the nation of Israel toward the Promised Land in Numbers 20:2-12. People gathered around Moses and quarreled with him because of their thirst when no water was available in the desert. Their murmuring aroused anger in Moses, and he impulsively disobeyed God.

God wanted to provide water for the Israelites and told Moses, "Speak to that rock before their eyes and it will pour out its water" (Numbers 20:8). Numbers 20:11,12 continues, "Moses raised his arm and struck the rock twice with his staff. Water gushed out, and the community and their livestock drank. But the LORD said to Moses and Aaron, 'Because you did not trust in me enough to honor me as holy in the sight of the Israelites, you will not bring this community into the land I give them.'"

It appears that Moses made a disastrous decision in anger. Just before he struck the rock, he said, "Listen, you rebels, must we bring you water out of this rock?" (Numbers 20:10b). Think of the difference it would have made in the future of this great man if he had only accepted God's intervention and had not reacted in anger and self-will. Moses missed the joyous entrance into the prosperous Promised Land with his family and his nation. A fit of anger may not keep you from heaven, but you may miss the joy of your salvation until you can react with patience and Christlike gentleness. James 1:20 says, "Man's anger does not bring about the righteous life that God desires."

DISASTER AVERTED FOR DAVID

In 1 Samuel 25, David accepted God's intervention and stopped before he killed a man in anger. David and his men guarded the livestock of a wealthy man named Nabal. At the time of sheep shearing, David expected Nabal to reward them with compensation. But Nabal replied, "Why should I take my bread and water, and the meat I have slaughtered for my shearers, and give it to men coming from who knows where? [and] . . . he hurled insults at them" (vv. 11,14).

David became so angry that he armed 400 of his men and started toward Nabal's home to kill him and the men of his household. One of Nabal's servants wisely told Nabal's wife, Abigail, "Think it over and see what you can do, because disaster is hanging over our master and his whole household" (25:17).

When Abigail saw David coming, she humbly bowed and asked forgiveness for Nabal's offense. She said, "When the

LORD has done for my master [David] every good thing he promised concerning him and has appointed him leader over Israel, my master will not have on his conscience the staggering burden of needless bloodshed or of having avenged himself" (vv. 30,31).

David saw the value of pausing and forgiving the offense of the person who had made him angry. He left it to God to take vengeance on Nabal. And 10 days later, the LORD struck Nabal and he died. David enjoyed the benefits of a clear conscience for not having allowed anger to dictate his actions. "Better a patient man than a warrior, a man who controls his temper than one who takes a city" (Proverbs 16:32).

WITHOUT WRATH

If you're tempted to express your anger in destructive ways toward another person, take a step back and enter into daily intercessory prayer that follows the pattern found in 1 Timothy 2:8: "I will therefore that men pray every where, lifting up holy hands, *without wrath* and doubting" (KJV, emphasis mine). God's will is for you to call the name of the person in prayer on a regular basis *until you no longer feel anger toward him or her.* Within 30 days the Holy Spirit will minister peace and love to your spirit that provides the foundation for healthy communication between you and the other individual.

LOOK TO JESUS

Inside or outside the home, when someone intentionally belittles you and takes a position against you, you are instructed by Jesus to "pray for those who persecute you" (Matthew 5:44, NIV). To help resolve strained relationships in your home, you may *ask God* to cause the individual to:

Be shown the truth about God's will and purpose in the situation.

Be persuaded that your motives are pure and that your life reveals the reality of your service to Christ.

Be convinced that his or her opposition to you is opposition to the will of Christ.

PAUSE, LOOK, PROCEED

When you find that anger is building up inside you toward an individual, consider taking the following steps:

1. Pause.

Pausing is a preventive measure. It can keep your emotions from taking over. It may keep you from doing or saying something rashly that will damage your relationship with the person or harm your spiritual and physical health.

2. Look.

Look at the situation thoroughly, and look for God's intervention and "way of escape" from possible disaster in your life.

3. Proceed.

Proceed with caution. "Let your gentleness be evident to all. The Lord is near. Do not be anxious about anything, but in everything, by prayer and petition, with thanksgiving, present your requests to God. And *the peace of God, which transcends all understanding, will guard your hearts and your minds in Christ Jesus*" (Philippians 4:5-7, emphasis mine).

BE ON ALERT

One day, two of my seven grandchildren, ages 5 and 7, got upset with each other about something. I was ready! I quoted a verse from Ephesians 4:32: "Be ye kind one to another, tenderhearted, forgiving one another, even as God for Christ's sake hath forgiven you" (KJV). These two little "angels" looked at me wide-eyed, like I thought I was God or something. At least it served to get their minds off their anger.

MAKE EVERY EFFORT

It is imperative that you try to stay free from feelings of anger in order to please God and to be able to genuinely experience loving relationships with others. "Make every effort to live in peace with all" (Hebrews 12:14, NIV). With the faithful help of the Spirit of God, you will be able to experience the joy of restoration and renewal in relationships where you have been troubled by feelings of anger.

LET'S PRAY

This is the beginning of the rest of your life. Your future does not need to be the same as your past. Would you pray this prayer with me? "Heavenly Father, I want You to help me face my anger. Forgive me for the times I have allowed anger to control me. Help me remember that things are going to work together for my good because of Your faithfulness to me. I am learning to trust in You more. I purpose to control my temper, instead of allowing my temper to control me. I forgive the person who hurt me, and I will show them it is so. In the name of our Lord Jesus Christ, Amen."

Hubert Morris is senior pastor of Evangel Temple Assembly of God in Monroe, Louisiana. He has served pastorates in North Carolina, New York, Georgia, and Missouri. A graduate of Evangel University in Springfield, Missouri, Morris served his alma mater for 15 years as vice president for institutional advancement and in other capacities. He also studied at Assemblies of God Theological Seminary. Morris served as the North Carolina District youth and Sunday school director. He and his wife, Glenda, have three daughters.

23

INFERIORITY

Building Your Self-Esteem

FRED MENDOZA

A deadly psychological virus is on the loose! It robs people of the quality of life they could be enjoying. It intimidates its victims from reaching their potential. It inhibits them from realizing their desired future. It incapacitates them from becoming successful, productive, and useful members of society. This deadly virus is inferiority—a feeling that has turned into a deadly complex.

Both psychology and the Bible offer answers. One offers insight; the other changes lives. I know. The answers in God's Word changed mine.

PSYCHOLOGICAL VIEW

Academic literature on inferiority complex is dominated by Alfred Adler (1870-1937), an Austrian psychiatrist, psychologist, and educator whose teachings on inferiority remain unsurpassed to this day. His simplistic definition of inferiority complex is "the inability to solve life's problems." His whole philosophy is summed up in the belief that "life is an unceasing struggle for superiority by a being who feels himself inferiorized." His main doctrine is that "behavior is determined by compensations for feelings of inferiority." In its wider version, this Adlerian psychological doctrine postulates the following:

Behavior is purposive and goal oriented: the goal is to overcome feelings of inferiority.

The desire for superiority is mainly a reaction to the feeling of inferiority.

Behavior is not necessarily dictated by a person's past experiences, as a person can decide to improve his present and future life regardless of unfavorable past experiences.

Behavior is calculated to compensate for feelings of inferiority that put down a person's sense of self-worth.

Compensations are thoughts, feelings, words, attitudes, actions, accomplishments, improvements, rewards, or the approval of others that are used to increase one's sense of self-worth.

When feelings of inferiority are adequately compensated, the feelings of inferiority subside.

When feelings of inferiority persist because they are not adequately compensated, they turn into inferiority complex.

SYMPTOMS

What are the symptoms of inferiority complex? Although one writer said, "Everything can be a symptom," here are some symptoms that are commonly associated with this complex:

Inability to meet the ordinary demands of living a healthy, happy, and productive life.

Self-devaluation.

Low perception of personal self-worth.

Self-rejection and even self-hate.

Feeling of chronic discouragement.

Persistent feelings of insecurity, guilt, shame, and anger.

Using one's power, wealth, education, or influence to assert superiority over other people.

Anger and jealousy toward others who are perceived to be better or superior.

Disassociation from other people who are perceived to be better or superior.

Undue calling of attention to oneself.

Putting down other people to feel important.

Trying to appear superior and knowledgeable by always being right.

Overreactions that give exaggerated importance to the least little setback.

Retreating before the most insignificant obstacle.

ROOT CAUSES

According to Adler, the causes of inferiority could be physical, psychological, or sociological. When a person feels inferior because of inborn or acquired physical defects—too short or too tall, too fat or too thin, cross-eyed, or any bodily deformity due to sickness or injury—his cause of inferiority feelings is physical.

When a person feels inferior because as a growing child he was unwanted, unloved, rejected, abused, and neglected by his parents or guardians, his inferiority feelings are psychologically induced. Conversely, a child could be inferiorized by being spoiled and pampered by his parents and learning to be irresponsible and overdependent upon others when he becomes an adult.

When a person isolates himself from others and becomes preoccupied with his feelings of inferiority as he unfavorably compares himself to others who possess more desirable physical, mental, and material assets, the cause of his inferiority feelings is sociological.

Consider these linear summaries:

> Self-perception . . . self-worth . . . self-esteem: Inferiority complex could be caused by a person's lack of healthy and proper self-esteem that comes from devaluating self-perception.
>
> Sense of impotence . . . insufficiency . . . insecurity . . . helplessness: Inferiority complex could result from a person's sense of total helplessness to solve life's problems.

While there are those who use their inferiority feelings as stepping-stones to a successful and meaningful life, unfortunately, there are those whose inferiority feelings turn into an inferiority complex. Why? Here are some possible reasons:

In childhood, they have been programmed by negative messages from others that they'll always be inferior. And they have internalized these messages.

As they grew up, repeated failures convinced them that they don't have what it takes to succeed in life.

Internalized negative messages and repeated failures as they were growing up have conditioned their minds to believe that they are destined to fail.

Consequently, they have given up hope to solve their life's problems.

PSYCHOLOGICAL APPROACH

Adler believed that in every lifestyle of failure, an inferiority complex can be found. How can an inferiority complex be overcome? Let's trace the steps to the Adlerian solution, before turning to God's Word. To begin with, all human beings have feelings of inferiority or a sense of inadequacy. Examples: A beggar feels financially inferior to a millionaire. A college freshman feels educationally inferior to his professor. A 90-pound man feels physically inferior to a Shaquille O'Neal. An ordinary citizen feels politically inferior to the nation's president. When a beggar, a college freshman, a physical weakling, or an ordinary citizen are motivated by their feelings of inferiority to compensate for their inferiority by improving their lot in life, their feeling of inferiority is actually working for their good.

Here's a summary of Adler's teaching on how to overcome abnormal feelings of inferiority:

Compensate for your areas of personal weakness by developing yourself in those areas or other areas to enhance your sense of self-worth.

Challenge your deeply ingrained irrational beliefs that make you think you cannot change and improve your life, and renew your thinking.

Be a contributing member of a community where your sense of self-worth is improved by serving and benefiting other people.

This psychological solution to the problem of inferiority complex is helpful, but the biblical teaching on how to overcome inferiority is more definitive and encouraging.

BIBLICAL TEACHING

As Christians, our sense of healthy self-worth and proper self-esteem is not based on the cultural criteria of self-worth: physical looks and prowess, level of IQ, educational attainment, material wealth or net worth, power, influence, prestige, and popularity. Rather, our sense of self-worth and self-esteem is based on God's gifts to us:

God created us in His own image and likeness (Genesis 1:26,27).

He loved us unconditionally even in our sinful and devalued condition before Him (Romans 5:6-8).

He paid for our redemption with a supreme price, the blood of His Son (1 Peter 1:18,19).

He extends to us the privilege of becoming members of His spiritual family (John 1:12,13).

He has given us everything we need to become holy or whole like Him (Ephesians 1:3-6; 1 Peter 1:15; 2 Peter 1:3,4).

He has made a radical change in us when He placed us in Christ (1 Corinthians 12:12,13; 2 Corinthians 5:17).

He has given us spiritual gifts with which to serve Him and others for His glory and for our fulfillment (1 Corinthians 12:7-11; Romans 12:6-8).

He has given us the ability to adjust and to adapt to any difficult situation (Philippians 4:10-13).

He has given us the Holy Spirit as a mark and a deposit that we belong to Him (Ephesians 1:13,14).

As Christians we are never helpless because we can face all the vicissitudes of life knowing that God is for us, not against us, and knowing that nothing can separate us from the love of God in Christ (Romans 8:28-39).

As Christians we can forget and leave our past behind and move on with God until we see Him face to face (Philippians 3:12-16,20).

Our feelings of inferiority can be changed to feelings of sufficiency, adequacy, and confidence in God by:

Seeing ourselves as God sees us in Christ.

Valuing ourselves as God values us in Christ.

Seeing our future as God sees our future in Christ.

Living in the power of God's Spirit who dwells in us.

Facing the challenges of life with the wisdom and the ability of God.

Discovering and using our spiritual gifts to serve God, the church, and the world.

I attest to the validity and applicability of these biblical principles for overcoming inferiority complex. Born to poor parents in a remote barrio in the Philippines, I was almost crippled psychologically by feelings of inferiority up to my teenage years. But God has enabled me to overcome my abnormal feelings of inferiority by improving my educational, economic, and social status through hard work and determination. More than this, God has done a redemptive reconstruction on my spirit, my soul, and my mind that rehabilitated me from abnormal feelings of inferiority. God even healed me when I was dying of typhoid fever at age 16 and called me to the ministry. My major victory over inferiority complex came when I was baptized in the Holy Spirit in 1957.

At age 31 in 1971, after planting three churches in the Philippines, I relocated to California with my wife, Perla, and our 5-year-old daughter, Naomi, to further my education. I'm older now, with university degrees in psychology and in education, with formal training in theology, and with a lifetime on-my-knees study of God's Word. God has blessed my life and ministry as a gospel radio broadcaster in the Philippines and as an Assemblies of God missionary from California to Singapore, where I served as president of Asia Theological Center for Evangelism and Missions for four years. Today, I'm leading a healthy and growing church in West Covina, California, which my wife, my daughter, and I started as a home Bible study 16 years ago. God has blessed us with a prime property, beautiful church facilities, a very talented and loving church family who are mostly professionals, and a Bible school for training home-grown ministry leaders.

The biblical cure for inferiority complex is encapsulated by Paul in Romans 12:1,2 where he teaches us to respond to

God's mercy by offering our bodies to Him—in whatever condition they may be—as a perpetual offering in an act of worship, and by renewing our minds in order to experience God's transformation in our lives. This renewing of our minds is done by replacing the carnal and worldly contents of our thought lives with the principles of God's Word.

If you are struggling with inferiority complex, here are sure ways to overcome:

Be born into God's family by receiving Jesus Christ as your Savior.

Derive your sense of self-worth and self-esteem from your personal relationship with God.

As a child of God, allow the Holy Spirit to change you day by day into the likeness of Christ.

Entrust to God your inborn physical and mental deficiencies that cannot be changed.

Ask God for grace to live with or to go through unchangeable life situations.

Reinterpret your life history in light of God's plan for you.

Put redemptive meaning and value to your painful life experiences.

Believe that you are not a helpless victim of your self-devaluating experiences in life.

Live your life with hope in view of Christ's return.

Always remember that in Christ you are somebody!

Think, speak, and act like you are really somebody in Christ.

This biblical approach to overcoming feelings of inferiority worked for me. It will work for you.

Fred Mendoza is the founding pastor of Charisma International Church in West Covina, California, and a member of the Board of Trustees for Vanguard University. He has served as president of Asia Theological Center for Evangelism and Missions in Singapore, during which time he was also associate pastor for the 5,000-member Calvary Charismatic Center. He has also served as associate pastor at First Assembly of God in Wilmington, California. Prior to that he pioneered three churches in the province of Pampanga in the Philippines, where he was also involved in gospel radio ministry. Mendoza and his wife, Perla, live in West Covina, California.

24

DEPRESSION

Free to Live Abundantly

LYNN WHEELER

In 20 years of full-time ministry (16 as an evangelist), I have never seen the spirit of depression run rampant like I am seeing today among God's people. I am not talking about people who do not serve God, but people who are doing their best to live for the Lord! In the second edition of their book *Happiness Is a Choice*, Frank Minirth and Paul Meier state, "Depression is America's #1 health problem." They further observe, "As psychiatrists we see more people suffer from depression than from all other emotional problems put together. A majority of Americans suffer from serious, clinical depression at some time during their lives. One American in twenty is medically diagnosed as suffering from depression. Depression is the leading cause of suicide. It occurs two times more often in females than males, and it occurs three times more often in higher socioeconomic groups."

A few years ago I personally went through a bout of depression. I knew what it was. I had studied it and preached about it for years. You go from feeling that everything is fine to not wanting to do anything. Even the things you love to do most become unimportant. I literally sat for hours just staring at the walls. Then you try to figure out a reason to live. The feeling of hopelessness and dejection is overwhelming.

The Bible says, "The thief comes only to steal and kill and destroy" (John 10:10, RSV). The enemy wants to take away your joy and destroy you. But Jesus said in the last half of that same verse, "I came that they [you] may have life, and have it abundantly."

Webster defines depression this way: "To be flattened vertically or dispirited." In Isaiah 61:3 (KJV), the prophet refers to a "spirit of heaviness." Here depression or discouragement is a spirit—a direct, diabolical attack of the enemy intended to destroy you. In the Hebrew it means to "put out the fire or grow dull." That is what depression will do to you.

In Isaiah 61:3, the prophet declares the alternative to the "spirit of despair" for the people of God. God wants to give you a "garment of praise instead of a spirit of despair" (NIV). So today, if you are battling depression, I encourage you to ask God to help you *change garments!*

All of the pamphlets and articles I have read on depression seem to agree on one thing: the quickest relief is provided by learning how to *think differently* about a given situation. The apostle Paul admonishes us about our thinking habits in Philippians 4:7,8: "The peace of God, which transcends all understanding, will guard your hearts and your minds in Christ Jesus. Finally, brothers, whatever is true, whatever is noble, whatever is right, whatever is pure, whatever is lovely, whatever is admirable—if anything is excellent or praise-worthy—think about such things."

What are you thinking about? Good or bad things? What you have or don't have? Blessings or curses? As long as we dwell on the negative, it will have an effect on our emotional lives. Set your mind on "good" and "godly" things.

Great people of God in the Bible went through times of depression. In fact, three men came to the point where they asked God to take their lives:

- Jonah: "Now, O Lord, take away my life, for it is better for me to die than to live" (Jonah 4:3).
- Moses: "If this is how you are going to treat me, put me to death right now—if I have found favor in your eyes—and do not let me face my own ruin" (Numbers 11:15).
- Elijah: "Elijah was afraid and ran for his life. When he came to Beersheba in Judah, he left his servant there, while he himself went a day's journey into the desert. He came to a broom tree, sat down under it and prayed that he might die. 'I have had enough, Lord,' he said. 'Take my life; I am no better than my ancestors'" (1 Kings 19:3,4).

These three men wanted to die. But God did not (and does not) mistake the moment for the man. We have all experienced times when we felt overwhelmed—mentally, physically, and spiritually exhausted. We have those days when we can relate to the French philosopher who said, "I have so much to do today, I must go to bed." Fatigue is a major cause of depression. When you get physically tired, it affects you mentally and emotionally.

Extended periods of time with rest can be healthy and move you from depression. In the Gospels we find Jesus pulling away for rest on several occasions. If we refuse Jesus' invitation to come apart and rest for a while we will eventually just come apart.

Over the last few years the most requested tape series from my ministry is entitled *All Stressed Up and No Place to Go.* One of the messages in that series is called "Dealing With Depression." The overwhelming response to this message was my first indication that a lot of Christians are struggling in this area. If you or someone you know is struggling with depression, please do not take it lightly. If it is not dealt with, it can result in broken homes, physical breakdown, spiritual breakdown, and suicide. I will always thank God for three friends who called me every day during my battle just to check on me.

How do we know if it is depression or a temporary setback? Again, I will share from personal experience. I withdrew from people, even close friends and family. I lost interest in the things I once loved. I found myself focusing on the negative things all the time. There was even a change in countenance and personality. If this is you, a friend, or family member, and you are still unsure, call a mental health service provider. Seek professional help.

There is also a scriptural solution to depression. Be honest. Pinpoint the cause and take it to God. He doesn't want you to live downcast and defeated. Musician and King David sobbed these same words three times in two chapters: "Why are you downcast, O my soul? Why so disturbed within me?" (Psalm 42:5; 42:11; 43:5). In every instance he gave his own answer: "Put your hope in God." By doing that, it wasn't long until he was saying, "Great is the LORD, and most worthy of praise" (48:1).

The prophet Isaiah makes reference to "the day the Lord gives you relief from suffering and turmoil and cruel bondage"

(Isaiah 14:3). Start today. With your willingness and God's help, you can rise out of depression.

I remember that feeling—as if I was in a deep dark pit. The constant inner turmoil was rooted in confusion. That confusion brought questions. What has happened to me? How did I get to this point? Why have some of my friends forsaken me? Will this ever be over? I had always known that God was able to help. I had preached it for years, prayed with people, and seen the power of God work miracles in their lives. But I had to believe it for me.

I will never forget the day I decided to change my "stinkin' thinkin'." I began to think on the good things of God. My blessings. My victories. I took my example from David who wrote these words in the midst of his depression: "My spirit grows faint within me; my heart within me is dismayed. I remember the days of long ago; I meditate on all your works and consider what your hands have done" (Psalm 143:4,5). Remembering and thinking about the good things of God can begin the process of stepping out of depression. The apostle Peter says, "And the God of all grace, who called you to His eternal glory in Christ, after you have suffered a little while, will himself restore you and make you strong, firm and steadfast" (1 Peter 5:10). Wow! God will not only restore us, but also make us strong, firm and steadfast. Praise the Lord!

In his book *Wisdom for Winning*, Mike Murdock presents the following five steps as a prescription for getting out of depression:

1. Understand that depression is no respecter of persons.
2. Recognize the danger of depression.
3. Find the basic cause and scriptural solution to your depression.

4. Take immediate action.

5. Practice three secrets of power living daily: (a) Respect the opinions of God concerning your life. (b) Habitualize your morning talks with God. (c) Faith talk, repeat out loud the viewpoint of God.

We must realize that depression is not a new attack from the enemy. There are many people in the Bible who suffered from depression. Jeremiah was so downcast he was going to leave the ministry (Jeremiah 9:2). The prophet Micah lost all confidence in people (Micah 7:4,5). Even the rich and wise Solomon confessed that he came to a place that he "hated life" (Ecclesiastes 2:17).

It is an old trick of hell still being used to sap the spirits of God's people. When that spirit of depression settles in, it even affects our church services. Don't allow the devil to use that old trick on you. Whatever it was that drove you to a state of depression, forget it. Don't dwell on it. Don't look back. You cannot go into your spiritual future looking in the rearview mirror. God says, "Forget the former things; do not dwell on the past. See, I am doing a new thing! Now it springs up; do you not perceive it? I am making a way in the desert and streams in the wasteland" (Isaiah 43:18,19).

Lynn Wheeler is a 1982 graduate of Central Bible College in Springfield, Missouri. He holds a B.A. degree in biblical studies. He served four years as youth pastor at Crossroads Cathedral in Oklahoma City, Oklahoma, under Pastor Dan Sheaffer. He has served as an evangelist for 16 years, traveling worldwide preaching crusades, camps, conventions, and retreats.

Wheeler has also been a contributing author for two other Onward books: Revival Sermons *and* Parenting.

25

NEGATIVITY

The Power of the Words We Speak

DARRELL YARBROUGH

He said, "Hi, I'm Ken, and I'm dying with AIDS. Am I welcome to come to church here?"

As quickly as I could get the words out of my mouth I answered, "You most certainly are: we're glad you're here." Then I hugged him and tears streamed down his face. He had an incurable disease and knew that his time was limited on this earth. Ken began to tell me about his past and the reason for the shape he was in. He told me his parents rejected him because of his homosexual lifestyle. He described how he fell so far in sin that he actually found himself in Los Angeles living on skid row as a male prostitute. Before me stood a man the world had chewed up and spit out. I wondered how God could use his life in a positive way. However, that morning I saw the power of God transform his life.

As I began to get to know Ken, I noticed that he never blamed God or anyone else for his condition. In fact, everything I heard him say was uplifting. The greatest thing I saw in Ken's life was that he never let it affect his speech. To his credit he would use his condition as an opportunity to tell others of the love of God. He told them how he was forgiven and set free from sin and its bondage. Many people were touched and won to the Lord by his willingness to speak frankly about the effects of sin.

Ken began to study for the ministry. And one day, while I was helping him prepare his first sermon, I noticed his health was beginning to deteriorate. He was entering the final stages of this horrible disease. Later, when I walked into his hospice room, I could sense an overwhelming peace. My wife and I were the only ones there as Ken left this life and entered the kingdom of heaven. However, Ken had made it clear to us he didn't want a lot of sadness when he died. This was a time for celebration; he was home and he was whole!

God taught me so much during my time with Ken. God showed me that what we say is so important, that there is power in the words we speak. Now, I'm not talking about simple positive confession. We know that just being positive about a situation doesn't change anything. The Word of God tells us, "Death and life are in the power of the tongue" (Proverbs 18:21, NKJV). Contrary to what you have heard, talk is not cheap. Talk is very expensive. We should know that our words are powerful. What we say affects others, and what they receive from us. When we speak the wrong word, it lessens our ability to see and hear the will of God for our lives.

In Matthew 12:37, Jesus said to the people of His day, "For by your words you will be justified, and by your words you will be condemned." Here Jesus was saying that inconsistency in the mouth will produce confusion in the man. In this verse, the Greek word for "word" refers to more than that which is uttered. It also refers to the thought, reason, or motive behind the word.

You can tell more about a person by what he says than by what is said about him. Even Jesus said, "Out of the abundance of the heart the mouth speaks" (Matthew 12:34). Ken never denied his situation was bad; however, he never let his situation dictate his future. Your words are a reflection of where you are going. In fact, your life largely reflects the fruit of your tongue. To speak life is to convey God's perspective on any issue you may face. To speak death is to declare life's negatives, to declare defeat, or complain constantly.

If you're a person who truly wants to turn a negative into a positive, you must first *be careful of the things you say*. What are you asking others to hear from your mouth? Are you constantly diminishing the power of God by your negative faith? A great Scripture to keep in mind is Ephesians 4:29: "Let no corrupt word proceed out of your mouth, but what is good for necessary edification, that it may impart grace to the hearers." The word "corrupt" literally means "decayed" or "rotten." We should never let anything that is rotten or spoiled come out of our mouths. Speak about the good things and blessings of God.

Second, *don't be afraid to speak to your circumstances*. So often we find it difficult to speak to circumstances, yet we speak to "things" every day. People talk to their televisions, to their appliances, to their plants, and even to themselves. Why do some people think it normal for us to speak to things, sometimes even in a negative way, yet belittle us when we decide to speak with God's authority and His Word, declaring that we are "more than conquerors"?

You must begin to speak to things that come against you. In doing so, you create a pattern to follow just like the one Jesus used when speaking to the fig tree. You can find it in Mark 11:14. Jesus said, "Let no one eat fruit from you ever again." When Jesus came to the tree and saw the leaves, He expected to find figs. When He didn't find figs it was as if the tree had lied. Notice that after He observed the tree, He did not speak to the leaves. He did not curse the figs. Jesus simply cursed the whole tree. The fact there were no figs on the tree was only an indication of a deeper problem.

Jesus spoke to an inarticulate object because it was not doing what God had created it to do. Many of us attack the symptoms of our circumstance instead of the real problem. In James 2:20 we are told, "Faith without works is dead." You see, talking about healing won't produce healing. Talking about prosperity won't produce prosperity. There must be more than just talking if lasting results are to be produced. Faith must accompany your words.[1]

Third, if you want to turn life's negatives into positives, you have to *believe that what God has said in His Word is true and that it is for you today*. You will experience troubles in life. You will face many obstacles that test your faith and resilience. But in John 16:33, Jesus said, "In the world you will have tribulation; but be of good cheer, I have overcome the world." That means God will never give up on you. You can put your trust in His promises. Remember what was said of the faith of Abraham: "He staggered not at the promise of God through unbelief; but was strong in faith, giving glory to God" (Romans 4:20, KJV).

Your personal happiness is influenced by the words that come out of your mouth. Your happiness does not hinge on your circumstances, financial status, health, or wealth. It hinges on the things in your heart that come out of your mouth. The Bible says, "A man has joy by the answer of his mouth, and a word spoken in due season, how good it is!" (Proverbs 15:23, NKJV). Make up your mind to enjoy this life on earth and to fulfill the destiny that God has for you. Stop looking at your circumstances and start speaking to your circumstances. Ken had every reason in the world to be unhappy and drown himself in self-pity and defeat. However, he determined he would give himself totally and completely to God and use what he had for His glory.

Finally, *there is power in what you say and there is also a lot of power in what you don't say.* Do you remember the old saying, "Actions speak louder than words"? How true that is even today. Don't forget that ignorance is always ready to speak first. The best time to say nothing is when you feel you must say something. You will never be hurt by what you don't say. Silence can be a weapon of power and is seldom disputed. Mark Twain said, "The difference between the right word and the almost right word is the difference between lightning and the lightning bug."[2] I heard someone say, "Your ears aren't made to shut, but your mouth is." If you want someone to forget your past or your mistakes, then quit talking about them. Stop bringing up what you want others to forget. Keep in front of you God's ability to forgive and forget your past. If He refuses to remember the mistakes that are under the blood of Jesus, why should you?

Take control of your mouth today. Begin to make every day count with God. Look at your negative circumstance and declare the power of God right now. Pray this prayer with me and begin to make this the first day of the rest of your life in *victory*:

"Dear Lord, I pray that You will take total and complete control of my speech. May I begin to declare the Word of God in my present situation. I refuse to dwell on the negative circumstances that are beyond my control and I place myself in the palm of Your hand. I ask that the power of the Holy Spirit be released around me right now. Cover me and lead me in Your will today. The Bible tells me that 'all things work together for good to those who love God, to those who are the called according to His purpose' (Romans 8:28). Therefore, I know that You are working all of my circumstances out for Your glory and my victory, which I receive now. I bless Your name and speak all of this in the name of Jesus Christ, Amen!"

Darrell Yarbrough is a graduate of Central Bible College, Springfield, Missouri. He has been honored by the National Register's Who's Who in Executives and Businesses for the past two years. He has traveled extensively throughout the country speaking in conferences and churches. He has been a frequent guest on the Trinity Broadcasting Network. Currently, he is pastor of La Palma Christian Center in La Palma, California. He and his wife, Kristen, have two daughters, Kathryn and Lauryn. He serves as presbyter of the Orange Section for the Southern California District of the Assemblies of God.

26

AGING PARENTS

Forget Me Not

JEFF SWAIM

It was 8:30 P.M. when the phone rang. It was my mother and she was frantic. "Jeff, please come over here, there are people in my house and they won't leave." I grabbed my coat and told my wife, Kathy, that I was racing over to Mom's house.

As I entered the house, Mom was crying. "Mom, what's wrong?" I asked.

"There are people in the other room and they won't leave," she replied.

"Where are they?" I asked.

Mom led me into the back bedroom.

"Where are they?" I repeated.

"Right there," she said, pointing to her old clothes hanging in the closet.

In disbelief, I reached out my arms and held her close to me. "Mom, it's going to be OK," I said, tears streaming down my face. My heroic and brilliant mother was living out a nightmare, having hallucinations brought on by a disease called Alzheimer's.

Even though Mom had been manifesting symptoms of Alzheimer's for years, which forced her to retire from teaching at Central Bible College after 28 years, I was not prepared for the cruel things my mom would experience. Her memories, her dignity, and her ability to distinguish reality were stolen from her.

Aging and death are inevitable. My father, for example, died suddenly on his 45th birthday. But, in some ways, it's more difficult to watch life eke out of a parent or grandparent. The days and months of bereavement and mourning can be stretched into years as we say a long good-bye to a parent. So, how does one press on when you find it difficult to look into the lifeless eyes of a dying or suffering parent?

The Bible gives us a wonderful foundation on which to stand when we face the inevitability of our parents' aging. It's found in a simple command: "Honor your father and your mother, so that you may live long in the land the LORD your God is giving you" (Exodus 20:12, NIV). The Lord is not merely speaking to rebellious teenagers in these verses. He is speaking to children of all ages. There are some principles we must commit to in order to give genuine honor to our father and mother.

We must have an *unchallenged* respect for our parents. Sometimes this respect is challenged because we resent how we were raised—perhaps in a dysfunctional home where love and tenderness were absent. I was fortunate to have a mother who continuously showed her love for God and her family. But others aren't as fortunate. They have to seek God's help in forgiving their parents. When we restore complete relationship, we will truly honor the Lord in His commandment of honoring our father and mother.

We must demonstrate an *unconditional* love to our parents. No matter how difficult the situation, our parents are still our parents. One person tried to comfort me by saying, "Jeff, just remember, that's not your mom." I replied, "Yes it is—every bit of her. For better or for worse in sickness and in health, I am bound with more than a vow. I'm commanded to honor her; she's still my mom."

We must *understand* the process of aging. Read books or search the Internet for information that will help you understand what your parent is going through with his or her ailment or declining health. I studied all I could on the symptoms of Alzheimer's, and it helped prepare me for what was ahead. It also enabled me to pray more specifically.

We must be willing to *unveil* the truth in order to receive help. I honored my mother in my heart and in my actions—to the point of denying at times that she had a problem. But by not admitting it, I couldn't help her. A newspaper article about President Ronald Reagan and his battle with Alzheimer's really spoke to me. The Reagan family was going through the same traumatic experience, and they decided to tell the world. All of a sudden, I knew it was OK to admit to people that my mom had Alzheimer's. I thought that Alzheimer's was some dark secret that families lived with when one of their members had been diagnosed with the disease. But, because of the Reagans' example, we began sharing the news so people could understand what was happening to her.

We must work to *do what's best for them*. From the onset of Mom's Alzheimer's there were signals that things were not normal. She would often repeat stories, her hair was not as neat, and she had trouble matching her clothes. Her inability to remember compromised her effectiveness to teach in the classroom and even to play the piano at church. I knew there was a problem when I heard her make a mistake on the piano; I had seldom heard her play a wrong note. She was a concert pianist, who could sight-read and transpose anything. And she had perfect pitch. She could also orchestrate pieces in her head. Her peers called her a musical genius. But, piece by piece, Mom's ministry and everyday life were evaporating with her diminishing cognitive ability. She had to give up teaching, writing and recording music, playing the piano at church, and, eventually, driving her car. She was becoming a prisoner.

Kathy and I tried our best to care for Mom while she lived in her own home. Kathy was constantly at Mom's house— three to four times per day. We attempted to help her eat right and take her medications. She came to our house several times a week for "grandma time." But the hallucinations became more frequent, which caused her to be up all hours of the day and night. Exhausted, she would fall asleep on the floor or just sitting in the corner. Finally we decided to put her in a nursing home. That was one of the most difficult decisions we ever made, but shortly thereafter we knew we had done the right thing. She was better off receiving constant care.

We must build *unforgettable* memories with our family. My wife and two girls played an amazing role in helping me through the valley of Alzheimer's. My wife demonstrated unconditional love day after day, visiting Mom and caring for her. When Mom received an award from the Music Hall of

Honor, my daughters received the award on her behalf. It was a proud, unforgettable moment for Stephanie and Lyndsey. They also grew in their faith as they dealt with their grandma's disease. Both of them felt compelled to write about their feelings while they were in high school. Stephanie wrote:

> My grandma does not remember me. In fact there is not a lot she does remember. She has Alzheimer's disease, and, as a result, lives in a nursing home. Alzheimer's is a cruel disease that has taken control of my grandmother's life. She can no longer do anything for herself; she must have assistance twenty-four hours a day. Although she lives but two miles from my home, I rarely visit her. It is hard for me to see her in her condition. For the rest of my life, I do not want to remember her not knowing who I am. I want to remember my grandmother, Winnie Swaim, before Alzheimer's: her humor, her laugh, her amazing musical talent, and her courage.
>
> My grandma was an amazing woman, and she is still my hero who has set an example for me to live up to. Her musical talents alone are what helped her raise three boys as a single parent. While raising her sons she worked on her undergraduate and graduate degrees in music at the University of Oregon, taught piano lessons to sixty-six students a week, and managed to graduate fifth in her class at the university. Grandma never once asked for help financially or acted like she needed it.
>
> She later influenced many lives as a music professor for twenty-eight years and she was given many

awards and accomplished numerous honorable tasks. She taught me that, if I set goals high enough, I could use my talents to achieve them and succeed.

The last $4^1/_2$ years of Mom's life, she didn't remember our names, yet she would tell us and everyone else that she loved them. To walk into her room at the nursing home was to walk into sunshine. Many of the workers at the nursing home would pass by her room just to hear her say, "I love you."

Seven months before Mom died, my youngest daughter, Lyndsey, went to visit her grandma by herself. She was determined to get Grandma to say her name. Lyndsey repeated her name over and over for several minutes, and then finally Grandma said, "Lyndsey."

Lyndsey wrote a poem about her experience:

ONE LAST TIME

Still alive, but her mind is halfway gone.
Her amazing life touched so many souls.
It seems she's gone, but to me she lives on.
To hear her say my name is my one goal.

I'd waited so many years to hear it,
How could someone I love forget my name?
My heart, hopeful, as by her side I sit,
She says, "I love you," but it's not the same.

My soul aches to watch my hero leave me,
Can you just say it; say it one last time?
It would mean so much to me can't you see?

Do you remember? Please give me some sign.
I love you Grandmother, my Grimsby.
Thank you God, she said it; she said, "Lyndsey."

—Lyndsey Swaim

During the last two years of Mom's life the only name we heard her say was "Jesus." Mom died on July 3, 2002. She suffered with Alzheimer's for more than 13 years. That evening one of her close friends of 35 years called and left a message on our answering machine to comfort us. She said, "I'm praying for you and your family, but I'm rejoicing with Winnie. She's out of her prison and home with Jesus." I played the message again and again and my smile grew wider and wider. Yes! Mom was indeed out of her prison. She was home with the Lord.

Since her death, I've often relied on Paul's prayer in 2 Corinthians 1:3-7. I'm confident It will encourage you as well as you deal with the issue of aging parents: "Praise be to the God and Father of our Lord Jesus Christ, the Father of compassion and the God of all comfort, who comforts us in all our troubles, so that we can comfort those in any trouble with the comfort we ourselves have received from God. For just as the sufferings of Christ flow over into our lives, so also through Christ our comfort overflows. If we are distressed, it is for your comfort and salvation; if we are comforted, it is for your comfort, which produces in you patient endurance of the same sufferings we suffer. And our hope for you is firm, because we know that just as you share in our sufferings, so also you share in our comfort."

Jeff Swaim is the director of the WorldHope project for Convoy of Hope. He is a noted conference and seminar speaker and has served in the National Youth Ministries department and the national Men's Ministries department (HonorBound). He is the author and co-author of more than a dozen youth and men's ministry resources with a particular focus on discipleship. He and his wife, Kathy, have two daughters: Stephanie and Lyndsey.

27

UNCERTAINTY

Finding God's Will

KEN HORN

"I have no will but that of God." —Brother Lawrence

Few of us can honestly say those words. But most Christians wish they could. There are two barriers to this: first, the barrier of our own willfulness that tends to oppose God's will; second, the barrier of not knowing God's will. This second barrier produces the question that, as a pastor, I was asked more than any other: "How can I know God's will?" The Bible provides abundant direction.

PREPARATION

Several things must occur before you can hope to accurately discern God's will for your life.

You must realize you can know God's will and that it is important to seek it. You must first be convinced of the fact that God wants you to know His will and that He will make it known to you. "You ought to say, 'If the Lord wills, we shall live and do this or that'" (James 4:15, NKJV).

You must be willing to obey. The lordship of Jesus Christ is important. Is He really your Lord? Or do you want Him primarily as a Savior, with none of the responsibilities? Knowing His will is dependent upon the answer to this question: Are you willing to do what He says no matter what?

Romans 12:1,2 must be a reality in your life: "Present your bodies a living sacrifice, holy, acceptable to God, which is your reasonable service. And . . . be transformed by the renewing of your mind, that you may prove what is that good and acceptable and perfect will of God." Until you are yielded to His lordship, you will likely fear God's will. But when you do make Him Lord, you will find that what you feared before is now "good and acceptable."

Jesus said, "If anyone desires to come after Me, let him deny himself, and take up his cross daily, and follow Me" (Luke 9:23). If you don't follow Him, you'll be too far away to know what He wants you to do. Realize too that God measures the sincerity of your heart. "Every way of a man is right in his own eyes, but the Lord weighs the hearts" (Proverbs 21:2).

You need to trust His will. It is always in your best interest to "commit your way to the Lord, trust also in him" (Psalm 37:5). Going your own way will lead to trouble. "Trust in the Lord with all your heart, and lean not on your own understanding; in all your ways acknowledge Him, and He shall direct your paths" (Proverbs 3:5,6).

When you know God's will and it looks difficult, go to Him for the strength you need to follow through. Pray as did the father of the demon-possessed son in Mark 9:24: "Lord, I believe; help my unbelief!"

You need to be listening. In the messages to the churches in Revelation 2 and 3, this admonition is repeatedly given: "He who has an ear, let him hear what the Spirit says to the churches." It is all too easy to "turn a deaf ear" to the promptings of the Spirit. We must be actively listening, making a concerted effort to hear what He is saying.

You need to pray. It is always important to pray specifically for any direction you need. "Be anxious for nothing, but in everything by prayer and supplication, with thanksgiving, let your requests be made known to God" (Philippians 4:6).

But what is more important is to "pray without ceasing" (1 Thessalonians 5:17) beforehand. When prayer is a way of life, it is easier to discern God's voice than if we only pray when we need to know His will. You most quickly recognize the voices of those with whom you spend the most time. Making prayer a way of life helps to make the voice of God recognizable.

With your heart adequately prepared, there are several places to look for God's direction.

THE WORD OF GOD

The Bible is God speaking to all who read it. It is full of general principles that apply to every believer. One need not seek special direction from God on an issue that is clearly addressed in Scripture. If the Bible says it, our responsibility is to obey without question. Jesus said, "If you hold to my teaching, you are really my disciples" (John 8:31, NIV).

ILLUMINATION

Most Christians have had the experience of a passage of Scripture "jumping out at them." This is the Holy Spirit shining God's light on it, saying, "This is for you!"

"Your word is a lamp to my feet and a light to my path. . . . The entrance of Your words gives light; it gives understanding to the simple" (Psalm 119:105,130, NKJV).

Begin Scripture reading by praying that the Holy Spirit would speak to you from it. It is this dynamic relationship with the Author of the Bible that brings home the reality that God's Word is "living and powerful, and sharper than any two-edged sword" (Hebrews 4:12). The Bible must not be read as a dead letter. It must be allowed to speak its living words into our lives: "The letter kills, but the Spirit gives life" (2 Corinthians 3:6).

THE HOLY SPIRIT'S INNER PROMPTINGS

John 16:13 promises that "the Spirit of truth . . . will guide you into all truth." One of the most common ways God speaks is through a "still small voice" (1 Kings 19:12).

Most Christians want God's will to be revealed in no uncertain terms. They wish God would speak dramatically, as He did to Moses out of a burning bush. But the fact is that He seldom shouts. The problem is we tend to fill our lives with other voices. Many homes find it impossible to turn the television off, even when no one is watching. Other noises crowd our days, making it nearly impossible to hear a "delicate, whispering voice" (as someone paraphrased 1 Kings 19:12). One needs to be quiet—and to find a quiet place. You can't hear that kind of voice when it is only one among many. Finding a place and time to listen every day is important.

If you have laid all the groundwork and are "walking in the Spirit" (Galatians 5:16), when you hear a voice of direction, you won't be asking, as so many do, "Is it God, me, or Satan?" You'll recognize God's voice.

GODLY COUNSEL

"The way of a fool is right in his own eyes, but he who heeds counsel is wise" (Proverbs 12:15). Much of the best counsel comes from the public ministry of men and women of God. Other counsel is personal.

When seeking counsel, it is important to seek out those who walk close to God. But no counselor is perfect. A counselor is not a decision-maker but a light-shedder. Ministries that specialize in "personal words" that authoritatively direct people's lives should be highly suspect.

"Plans fail for lack of counsel, but with many advisers they succeed" (Proverbs 15:22, NIV). This doesn't mean you accept everything they say. In fact, two godly counselors may disagree; but it may be important for you to hear two sides. That's why "in a multitude of counselors there is safety" (Proverbs 24:6, NKJV). Anything a counselor says, no matter how godly the individual, must be weighed before God. He must make the final decision.

GOD-GIVEN ABILITIES

Recognizing that "our sufficiency is from God" (2 Corinthians 3:5), we should also realize that those talents God has given us should be used to give Him glory. But we cannot say, just because we lack an ability needed for a particular ministry, that God does not want us involved in it. Perhaps the gift is dormant, or God may want to take you beyond your strengths. He specializes in using "weak members" (see 1 Corinthians 12:22). "Whatever you do," advises Paul, "do all to the glory of God" (1 Corinthians 10:31).

CIRCUMSTANCES

Circumstances are the most often used and the least important means for determining God's will. Jesus had harsh words for those seeking a sign (Matthew 12:39). Though He did signs and wonders, He never did them on command. Putting a "fleece" before the Lord is based on one biblical episode (Judges 6:36-40) and is not taught as a regular way to determine God's will.

One of the greatest barriers to knowing God's will is what I call Christian fatalism. Lazy Christians typically say things like, "If God wants it to happen, it will happen," shunning their responsibility. In the words of the old song, "Que será será. Whatever will be will be." If there are problems, they say, "The door's shut."

But many times, it's not. It just appears that way. Paul said, "For a great and effective door has opened to me, and there are many adversaries" (1 Corinthians 16:9). Many would have said, "The door is closed in Ephesus." But Paul saw an open door with "many who oppose me" (NIV). Christians too often stop short of God's perfect will because a situation looks difficult. *The door's closed,* they think, when, in reality, it is wide open and Satan has jammed the doorway with adversaries to keep the Christian out. God's way is seldom the easiest way. The devil invests a lot of energy throwing obstacles in the way of doors God has opened. He wants to convince you they are closed.

Jesus is "He who opens and no one shuts, and shuts and no one opens." He says, "I have set before you an open door, and no one can shut it" (Revelation 3:7,8, NKJV). It is tragic when a believer turns away from an open door simply because he has been opposed by Satan. Romans 8:28 assures us that all circumstances "work together for good to those who love God." Speaking of his imprisonment, Paul said, "What has happened to me has really served to advance the gospel" (Philippians 1:12-14, NIV).

Sometimes the reverse is true. What seems to be an open door is, in reality, one God does not want you to walk through. Earl Beaconsfield said, "Next to knowing when to seize an opportunity, the most important thing is to know when to forego an advantage."

God can and does arrange circumstances, and they should be weighed. But circumstances, whether good or bad, must never stand alone in determining God's will.

WHEN GOD SEEMS SILENT

But what if you need to make a decision and have not heard from God? You are told to "love the Lord your God . . . with all your mind" (Matthew 22:37, NKJV). God also says, "Come now, and let us reason together" (Isaiah 1:18). Use the mind, the logic, God has given you. Reason through the pros and cons of each decision, then make the best informed decision possible.

Before implementing that decision, talk to God. "God, I have sought Your will, but have not heard clearly from You.

This is what seems best to do. If this is wrong, please let the Holy Spirit check me." I've never known God to let someone make a mistake who honestly prayed this.

THE AFTER-TEST

When you have found God's will and implemented it, there should be peace. His peace "surpasses all understanding" (Philippians 4:7), regardless of what God has asked you to do.

Ken Horn, D.Min., is managing editor of Today's Pentecostal Evangel, *and an adjunct professor at Assemblies of God Theological Seminary. He has been a pastor and missionary evangelist.*

Endnotes

Chapter 4

1. Maggie McKinney, "Return to the Future," My Turn, *Newsweek*, March 6, 1995.
2. McKinney.

Chapter 13

1. Elisabeth Kubler-Ross, *On Death and Dying* (New York: Maxwell Macmillan International, 1993). While the book deals primarily with death and dying, the five stages of grief have been widely accepted as a way to understand what one experiences in other situations where individuals suffer loss.
2. In this chapter only representative references will be given from the Book of Job to show how he went through the five stages of grief. Covering the entire Book of Job to demonstrate

the stages of grief would require a study of the whole book and is beyond the purpose of this chapter.

3. For some Christians the word *anger* is viewed as *sin*. As a result, in counseling they are more willing to admit emotions such as frustration and disappointment. But these emotions are really anger. It is important to understand that anger in itself is not sin. It is the improper response to anger that is sin.

Chapter 22

1. H. Maurice Lednicky, *Faded Glory* (Springfield, Missouri: Lifestyle Ministries, 2002), 155.

Chapter 25

1. Stan Fortenberry, *From Valium to Victory* (Praise Books, 1989).
2. John L. Mason, *You're Born an Original, Don't Die a Copy* (Insight International, 1993).

About the Editors

George O. Wood is general secretary of the Assemblies of God. The son of missionary parents to China and Tibet, he holds a doctoral degree in pastoral theology from Fuller Theological Seminary, a juris doctorate from Western State University College of Law, and membership in the California State Bar. He is the author of several books, including *Living Fully: The Successful Life*, *A Psalm in My Heart*, and a college text on the Book of Acts.

Dr. Wood formerly served as assistant superintendent for the Southern California District of the Assemblies of God and pastored 17 years at Newport-Mesa Christian Life Center in Costa Mesa, California. Dr. Wood and his wife, Jewell, have two children, Evangeline and George Paul.

Hal Donaldson is editor in chief of *Today's Pentecostal Evangel*, the official voice of the Assemblies of God and the largest Pentecostal magazine in the world. Donaldson also serves as founder and president of Convoy of Hope, a nonprofit ministry that conducts humanitarian/evangelism efforts across America and around the world. Through Convoy of Hope, millions of needy families have received groceries, Bibles, medical attention, and job opportunities. And many have found Jesus Christ and been assimilated into local churches.

Donaldson is the author of 19 books, including: *One Man's Compassion* (the Mark Buntain story), *Treasures in Heaven* (the Huldah Buntain story), *The Vow*, *Pleasing God*, *Where Is the Lost Ark?*, and *Parenting*. A graduate of Bethany College, where he served as an instructor, Donaldson also has a B.A. in journalism from San Jose State University. He and his wife, Doree, have four daughters: Lindsay, Erin-Rae, Lauren and Haly.

Ken Horn is managing editor of *Today's Pentecostal Evangel* and an adjunct professor at Assemblies of God Theological Seminary, both in Springfield, Missouri. He received his bachelor's degree from Bethany College of the Assemblies of God, M.A. from Simpson College, D.Min. from California Graduate School of Theology, and did additional graduate work at Golden Gate Theological Seminary. Horn pastored three churches in California and Oregon. He has taught theology and related subjects on the graduate and undergraduate levels at Simpson College and other institutions. His published books include *Revival Sermons* and *Living Like Jesus*. He and his wife, Peggy, traveled as missionary evangelists in Eastern Europe in the 1980s.

Order Information

For a complete list of books
offered by Onward Books, Inc.
and an order form, please call or write:

Onward Books, Inc.
4848 South Landon Court
Springfield, MO 65810
417-890-7465

e-mail address:
onwardbooks@aol.com

Or visit our Web site at:

www.onwardbooks.com